Anonymous

San Rafael Cook Book

Anonymous

San Rafael Cook Book

ISBN/EAN: 9783744795838

Printed in Europe, USA, Canada, Australia, Japan

Cover: Foto ©Lupo / pixelio.de

More available books at **www.hansebooks.com**

1898

San Rafael Cook Book

COMPILED BY THE

Ladies of San Rafael

San Rafael,   California

Preface.

"We may live without poetry, music, and art;
We may live without conscience, and live without heart;
We may live without friends; we may live without books;
But civilized man cannot live without cooks.
He may live without books,—what is knowledge but grieving?
He may live without hope,—what is hope but deceiving?
He may live without love,—what is passion but pining?
But where is the man that can live without dining?"

ADVERTISEMENT.

SAN RAFAEL & S. F. EXPRESS

We transport our

Furniture, Pianos, Baggage and Freight

BY TEAM WITHOUT CHANGE

In a SPECIAL CAR by broad gauge train between San Rafael and San Francisco.

San Rafael Office,
819 FOURTH ST.
Telephone Black 22.   bet. C and D

S. F. Office,
323 EAST ST. . . Telephone 496.

OSCAR FITCH,
FRED H. CARROLL,
Proprietors.

The Jordan House

San Rafael, Cal.

•———— Firstclass ————•

Family Boarding-House

SIXTH ST., HEAD OF B.

Beautiful View.   Fine Grounds.

MRS. J. F. JORDAN,
Proprietress.

KURTZ & MAYER

San Rafael

Supplies for Parties a Specialty

French Bakery
AND .. Confectionery....

Hotels, restaurants, and families supplied at shortest notice . . . .
All kinds of wedding cake made to order . . . .

CORNER
D AND SECOND STS.

Bread.

Rules for Making Bread.

Twice as much flour as wetting is a good rule to follow, to avoid having the bread too stiff. By this rule, beat with a spoon for 20 minutes, and let stand over night. In the morning add as little flour as possible to mold into loaves.

For 4 large loaves, take 3 pints of liquid, ($\frac{1}{2}$ fresh milk and $\frac{1}{2}$ potato water); in warm weather $\frac{1}{2}$ cake of yeast, and 3 quarts of flour, 1 tablespoon sugar, same of butter or lard, and salt.

In cold weather more yeast is required.

Bread is better when raised slowly.

Bread should never fall, but be mixed before reaching this stage.

Before putting into the oven, cut across the top 3 times; for a rich brown crust nothing equals melted butter, for brushing. The oven must be hot when the bread is put in, and after it is well browned a more moderate oven will do. Bake bread from $\frac{1}{2}$ to 1 hour, according to size of loaf, and always in separate pans.

POTATO YEAST.—*Mrs. Geo. M. Dodge.*

Peel and grate 3 medium sized raw potatoes; pour 1 quart of boiling water over them, stirring well all the time. Let it stand on the back of the stove, and add 1 tablespoon sugar, and a little salt. When luke-warm, add $\frac{1}{2}$ a cup of baker's yeast or one cake of compressed yeast dissolved in $\frac{1}{2}$ cup water. Let it stand in a warm place in open stone jar until it ferments. Then cover and set away in a cool place, and it is ready for use. This yeast will keep 2 or 3 weeks in cool weather.

TO MAKE YEAST WITHOUT LEAVEN.—*Mrs. Geo. Bunn.*

In 2 quarts of water let 2 ounces of hops boil for $\frac{1}{2}$ hour; strain the liquid, and let it stand in a wide earthenware bowl. When luke-warm add a small quantity of salt—say $\frac{1}{2}$ handful—and $\frac{1}{4}$ pound of sugar. Take some of the liquor, and well mix up in it $\frac{1}{2}$ pound of the best flour, beating this up thoroughly in the whole afterwards. The next day but one, put in 1$\frac{1}{2}$ pounds of boiled and mashed potatoes; let it stand one more day, after which it may be bottled for use. It should be kept near the fire while making, so as to keep it about the temperature of new milk; and it should also be frequently stirred during the process of making. When bottled, it should be kept in a cool place.

BREAD.

SIMPLE MANNER OF MAKING GOOD BREAD.—*Mrs. Wm. Alexander.*

½ cake of compressed yeast; 2 medium sized potatoes, with water in which they were boiled, about 1 quart; 1 tablespoon white sugar; 1 tablespoon shortening. Mix the above at night in as much flour as is required to make a stiff dough; cover and let stand until morning. Knead well at night, and also in the morning. Let it rise again in morning, before putting in pans. The water for bread, including potato water, should be 1 quart. The above will make 3 nice sized loaves.

BREWERS' YEAST BREAD.—*Mrs. W. J. Wickman.*

Take 1 quart brewers' yeast, put it in a pitcher and allow it to settle; pour off all but the sediment and add 1 quart of water, and allow it to settle again. Pour off the top again, and re-cover with another 1 quart of water, and allow it to settle. Again pour off the water and save the settlings. Into this put a small amount of sugar, about 1 tablespoonful, or to taste; salt to taste, and 1 or 1½ pints of water at blood heat. Stir this into the middle of about 2 quarts of flour. Mold well and allow to rise 1 or 1½ hours; when light, mold into pans and bake 1 hour.

RYE BREAD.—*Mrs. McMahon.*

Make a sponge of 1 quart warm water and ½ cake of yeast; thicken with rye flour; set in warm place to rise. When light, add 2 cups of wheat flour, and then rye flour to make thick enough to mold; let rise, and bake about 1 hour in a moderate oven.

WHOLE WHEAT BREAD.—*Mrs. W. F. Jones.*

1 pint of milk, 1 pint of water, both warm, 1 cup of syrup, 1 teaspoon of salt, 1 teacup of white flour, ¾ of a cake of yeast in winter and ½ in summer, and about 2 quarts of whole wheat flour. It should be a stiff batter; cover and let stand over night. In the morning, stir well and turn into 2 good sized bread pans without kneading. Bake when light from ¾ of an hour to an hour in a moderate oven.

CINNAMON BUNS.—*Mrs. A. A. Curtis.*

Make a sponge of 1 pint of sweet milk, 1 heaping cup of lard, ½ pint of yeast, ½ cup of sugar, 1 quart of flour; set at night. In the morning add 2 eggs beaten light, and salt; make up stiff as for bread. When light divide in two parts, roll out about an inch thick, and narrow; spread with the mixture, and roll as for jelly cake; cut in slices; lay in pan to rise again; bake 20 minutes.

MIXTURE.—1 pound of butter, browned to a rich brown; when cool add enough sugar to absorb the butter, and about 2 tablespoons of water; add enough sugar to absorb both water and butter; flavor with cinnamon.

RUSKS.—*Mrs. W. F. Jones.*

1 pint of new milk, 1 cup of sugar, ⅔ cup of butter, 2 eggs, 1 quart of flour. Cream the butter and sugar, beat the eggs well and add to them the tepid milk. Mix and add the sifted flour, beating well. Then dissolve 1 cake of yeast in a little tepid water or 1 cup of potato yeast,

and stir into the sponge. Put in a warm place until morning. Then add enough flour to knead on the board and let rise again. When light make into round biscuit and drop in the center of a muffin ring, and when light bake a delicate brown. Before putting into the oven brush with melted butter.

PARKER HOUSE ROLLS.—*Mrs. W. J. Dickson.*

Boil 1 pint of milk with butter about the size of an egg. When cool add 1 teaspoon salt, ½ cup yeast, and flour enough to make a thick batter; stir well. When light, knead fifteen minutes; roll out, cut with a large cutter, spread with butter, fold over, put in the pans, and when light, bake in a quick oven.

BOSTON BROWN BREAD.—*Mrs. W. F. Jones.*

1 coffee cup corn meal, 1 coffee cup graham, 1 coffee cup white flour, ½ coffee cup molasses, 2 coffee cups sour milk, 1 teaspoon salt, 1 heaping teaspoon soda and 1 of baking powder sifted with the white flour. Steam 3 hours in a funnel steamer.

BOSTON BROWN BREAD.—*Mrs. E. A. Hartman.*

Made in a minute, and sure to be good; never fails! 1 cup of molasses, 2 cups of cold water, 2 teaspoons of soda, and mix. Stir this mixture into 2 cups of white flour and 2 cups of graham flour. Boil in pudding pail 3 hours.

RAISED MUFFINS.—*Mrs. Geo. M. Dodge.*

1 cup sweet milk scalded and a small piece of butter melted in it. Add to this enough flour for a stiff batter, a little salt, 1 tablespoon of sugar and ½ cup of yeast. Beat well and let it rise over night. In the morning beat in one egg and let it rise again in gem pans for about 20 minutes. Bake 15 minutes.

WHOLE WHEAT MUFFINS.—*Mrs. McMahon.*

Make batter of 1 pint sweet milk, 1 teaspoon sugar, 1 of salt, 1 tablespoon butter, ½ cup of yeast; add flour enough to make a thin batter; let rise. When light, add 2 well-beaten eggs and ½ teaspoon soda; let stand ½ hour to rise. Bake in quick oven.

MUFFINS.—*Mrs. W. F. Jones.*

½ cup of sweet milk, 2 eggs, 1 tablespoon sugar, melted butter the size of an English walnut, salt, 1 teaspoon baking powder sifted with 1½ cups of flour. Bake quickly until a light brown.

WAFFLES.—*Mrs. A. A. Smith.*

2 eggs beaten separately, ¾ cup of melted butter, 4 cups of flour, 2 teaspoons of baking powder, milk sufficient to make a thin batter. 3 tablespoonfuls to a medium sized waffle iron. Be sure and have the iron well greased on both sides and very hot. Excellent.

RICE GRIDDLE CAKES.—*Mrs. W. F. Jones.*

Beat 2 eggs light, stir in 1 cup of boiled rice, 1 tablespoon sugar, ½ teaspoon of salt, and 2 cups sour milk. Lastly sift in 1 cup of flour, 1 teaspoon soda and 1 teaspoon yeast powder. If a trifle too stiff, add a little milk; or if too thin, add a little more flour.

GRIDDLE CAKES.—*Mrs. Daniel Bradford.*

1 pint of sour milk, 1 pint of flour, mix and let stand over night. In the morning add ½ teaspoon of soda and 2 eggs well beaten. Cook on hot griddle.

CREAM BISCUIT.—*Mrs. Daniel Bradford.*

2 cups of flour, ½ cup of sweet cream, 2 teaspoons of baking powder sifted with the flour; salt; a little milk to make soft dough to roll out.

DROP BISCUIT.—*Mrs. W. F. Jones.*

1 quart of flour sifted with 3 heaping teaspoons baking powder, and 1 teaspoon of salt. Rub in a piece of butter the size of an egg, and then stir in 1 pint of sweet milk. Drop from a spoon on buttered tins, and bake in a quick oven.

BAKING POWDER BISCUIT.—*Mrs. W. F. Jones.*

Sift 3 heaping teaspoons baking powder and a little salt with 1 quart of flour, and rub in ½ cup of butter. Then wet with milk sufficient to roll. Cut in small biscuit, brush with melted butter, and bake in a quick oven.

SALLY LUNN.—*Mrs. Daniel Bradford.*

1 quart of flour and 2 teaspoons of baking powder well mixed, 3 large spoons of sugar put in the flour, salt, ½ cup of cream, or butter size of an egg, 2 cups of milk, 2 eggs not beaten. All stirred together. This makes 2 cards.

POPOVERS.—*Mrs. J. E. Alexander.*

Beat 2 eggs just enough to mix, add 1 cup milk and 2 level cups flour; beat 5 minutes; add 1 teaspoon salt and another cup of milk; beat 10 minutes more and bake in quick oven.

FAVORITES.—*Mrs. E. B. Mahon.*

1½ cups of milk, 1 cup of flour, 1 teaspoonful of butter, 2 eggs beaten separately; melt the butter and put into the milk and beaten yolks, a pinch of salt, whites well beaten put in last. Bake ½ hour in gem pans.

CORN BREAD, OR JOHNNY CAKE.—*Mrs. W. F. Jones.*

1 egg, 6 tablespoons corn meal, 3 tablespoons flour, 3 tablespoons sugar, 1 teaspoon of baking powder, and 1 teaspoon of soda sifted with the flour. A pinch of salt, ½ cup of sour cream, and ½ cup sour milk. If you have no sour cream use 1 cup of sour milk and a heaping tablespoon melted butter. This can be made with sweet milk and 2 teaspoons of baking powder, but it is not so nice.

CALEDONIAS.—*Mrs. Tharp.*

1 cup yellow cornmeal, 1½ cups flour, 1 teaspoonful Royal baking powder, 1 tablespoonful lard, a little salt. Mix well, as you would for breakfast rolls. Then add 1 cup of half milk and half water. Mix into

a paste, and roll out thin, cutting into rather small rounds. Fry in boiling lard. Serve hot. Pull open and spread with butter.

DEVILED HAM ROLLS.—*Mrs. Tharp.*

Make light, rather rich pastry, roll thin and cut in squares of about 4 inches. Spread upon each square a small quantity of deviled ham, leaving about ½ inch around the edges uncovered. Moisten the edges with cold water, and roll each square compactly. Press ends together, brush over with white of egg, and bake.

GRAHAM GEMS.—*Miss H. Pregge.*

1 cup of sweet milk, 1 egg, 1 tablespoon sugar, a little salt, 3 teaspoons of baking powder, and graham flour sufficient for a thin batter.

CREAM TOAST.—*Mrs. E. B. Mahon.*

Put 2 pieces of buttered toast in a hot dish, boil ¾ cup of milk, add ½ teaspoon of butter, season with a pinch of salt, and add sugar if liked. Mix the yolk of an egg with ¼ cup of cream; add slowly the boiling milk to the cream and yolk, stirring constantly. Pour over the toast.

ADVERTISEMENT.

Now you are through with your Bread,
So before you get souped
Go to Lorellard & Bratt's,
Where you never get duped.

Their Photographs Are equal to the best you can obtain in the City. You no longer need to take the train and journey with best gowns and children when you can step in at home while you are feeling bright, fresh, with hair nicely arranged and an expression of happiness, having all the attention and time desired in arranging positions, etc.

They will give you the very latest styles in carbon, platina or Gloss. They make a specialty in residence and outdoor groups.

Work done on short notice, and orders filled promptly, guaranteeing work that will not fade. Call and see samples.

Studio 606 1=2 Fourth St.
San Rafael.

Orders Promptly Attended to.

Fourth St , near B,
San Rafael.

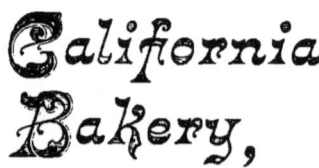

BREAD AND FANCY CAKES.—

GENUINE MILK AND RYE BREAD

Ph. Vogel,
Proprietor.

Soups.

Rules for Stock.

Put meat to cook in cold water; simmer slowly not less than 5 hours, skimming occasionally.

A piece of liver is an addition: or cooked meat or cooked bones will give the rich brown color without the use of burnt sugar.

CARAMEL FOR COLORING SOUP.

Melt 1 cup white sugar in a saucepan till it is dark: add slowly 1 cup of cold water, stirring briskly, and boil till it thickens. Keep in large mouthed bottle.

TO CLEAR SOUP.

When hot add the well-beaten white of an egg, and as the soup boils up, after stirring in the egg, skim well.

All milk soups are improved by the addition of cream.

BOUILLON.—*Mrs L. A. Lancel*

Take from 4 to 5 pounds of beef, cover with cold water, add salt. When boiled, skim and add ½ teaspoon of black pepper, 2 carrots, 2 turnips, 2 leeks, celery and parsley; boil from 4 to 5 hours, strain, and set aside. When to be used, roast one good sized onion dry, in the oven; stick whole cloves in it; put in the stock and boil 10 minutes. If liked, add half a glass of sherry.

MARROWBALLS FOR SOUP.—*Mrs. W. F. Jones.*

Chop fine ½ cup of marrow good and fresh, and rub with it 1 cup of flour and a saltspoon of salt. Wet with sufficient cold water to make like pastry, and roll into tiny balls like small marbles. Drop into boiling soup, boil 15 to 20 minutes, and serve.

OXTAIL SOUP.—*Mrs. W Fraser.*

Chop an oxtail in slices and fry a nice brown in butter. Add 3 quarts water, 1 carrot, a small piece turnip, 1 onion, 1 stick of celery, and a little salt and pepper. Let simmer 5 hours, strain through colander, add a little rice, and leave in a few pieces of the oxtail. Let simmer until rice is done, then serve.

OXTAIL SOUP.—*Miss H. Pregge.*

Separate the joints of 2 oxtails; put them into a frying pan with a little butter and fry them nice and brown: add 1 onion and 1 carrot and fry brown also. Then put all into a soup kettle with about 3 quarts of water, let it simmer slowly, add a few cloves and a blade of mace, also a little barley, and cook well. If desired add a little sherry wine just before sending to the table.

CREAM OF BARLEY SOUP.—*Mrs. E. W. Newhall.*

1½ pints strong chicken broth or stock, ½ cup barley, 1 cup cream, yolks of 4 eggs; flavor with celery, lemon or onion. Wash the barley thoroughly, and cook slowly until soft enough to rub through a sieve. Put it into the strained chicken broth, and cook half an hour. Then add the yolks of 4 eggs, well beaten. Be sure and pour the broth on to the eggs, not the eggs into the broth. Lastly add one cup of cream. Do not boil after the cream is added. If too thick, add a little hot milk to the right consistency, and salt to taste.

CREAM OF CELERY SOUP.—*Mrs. W. F. C. Hasson.*

This receipt is also good for cauliflower, potato, or asparagus. If you have roast beef bones left from the day before, break them up and put on to boil with soup greens and a head of celery. (If you have no bones, and do not wish to buy fresh soup meat, water alone will do, but it will not be as savory.) Add some young onions, 5 or 6, a tablespoon of butter, and some flour dissolved in water until smooth, and when the soup is boiling add the flour, salt, pepper, a little mace, and the top slice of a lime for a few minutes only, as it will make the soup bitter if left longer. For potato soup, leave out the mace and lime, but add a pinch of allspice instead. After the celery is quite soft, strain it through a fine sieve, add a gill of cream thinned out in as much milk, and the yolk of 1 egg, all beaten and allowed to come to a boil. Serve with fried bread cut in slices. For asparagus or cauliflower, cut off the heads and boil only the stalks before straining, as they have to be all mashed through the strainer; then put in the heads and flower, and let boil in the soup until tender.

CREAM OF RICE SOUP.—*Mrs. W. F. Jones.*

Fry 1 cup of rice in 1 tablespoon of butter until the rice turns white, then add 2 quarts of boiling milk, and cook slowly, stirring occasionally until done. Pass through a fine wire sieve by mashing with a spoon. Season with salt and grated nutmeg; or instead of the nutmeg, cut up a small onion, and fry with the rice. Add 1 cup of cream just in time to warm but not boil, before serving. Lastly, add squares of bread fried in butter. Part stock or chicken broth may be used instead of all milk. If too thick, thin with milk to the right consistency.

MOCK TURTLE SOUP.—*Mrs. Herbert Kellogg.*

Have a good stock. Boil 1 quart of dark beans in water until tender, and mash through colander. Add a pinch of cloves, allspice and black peppers bruised and tied in a cloth; add the stock. Chop 3 hard boiled eggs and place in the tureen; pour the soup over, and add ½ glass of sherry at the last. Salt to taste.

SOUP.

BLACK BEAN SOUP.—*Mrs. W. F. Jones.*

2 cups of black beans boiled until tender. Mash through a colander, and add to 1 quart of rich stock; when hot, strain through a sieve; season with allspice, cloves, pepper and salt. Just before serving, add a cup of cream. This is far more delicate than where pork is used. Fry squares of bread in butter until they are a rich brown, and add last.

WHITE BEAN SOUP.—*Mrs. W. F. Jones.*

Put 1 cup of white pea beans to cook, and when tender mash through a colander and add milk until of the right consistency. Season with salt and pepper; and thyme fresh from the garden is preferable to the powdered. Tablespoon of butter and 1 cup of cream. Serve with squares of bread fried brown in butter.

ONION SOUP (JOE TILDEN'S.)—*Mrs. W. F. C. Hasson.*

4 large onions cut up, 6 ounces butter, salt, cayenne, stock and milk, yolks of 4 eggs, ¼ loaf of French bread cut in very thin slices and dried, and 2 tablespoons grated Parmesan cheese. Slowly stew the onions in the butter for 1 hour, stirring frequently and being careful not to burn. Add salt, pepper, cayenne, and stock, and cook one hour; add ½ as much milk as stock. Have in the tureen the bread and cheese; beat up the eggs and mix with them a ladleful of the soup. Pour this on the bread, cover close for five minutes, let stand, add the rest of the soup, and serve at once.

PUREE OF PEAS.—*Mrs. McMahon.*

1 quart fresh peas, 2 cups boiling milk, 1 small minced onion, 2 tablespoons butter rubbed up with 1 of flour; pepper and salt, handful of dry bread crumbs, 1 cup of boiling water. Put peas and onions over the fire with the hot water; boil half an hour; strain and rub through a sieve, working peas to a pulp. Meanwhile boil milk, butter, and flour, also pepper and salt; stir in bread crumbs, and one minute later the thickened milk. Serve at once.

TOMATO BISQUE.—*Mrs. Geo. Bunn.*

1 quart cooked tomatoes, 2 quarts sweet milk, 1 level teaspoon cornstarch, salt, butter, paprika or white pepper, 1 teaspoon soda. Strain the tomatoes and put on to heat; when boiling put in soda, then add the hot milk, sugar, salt, pepper, and butter. Cook the cornstarch in milk before adding to tomatoes, to prevent curdling. Some prefer a little sugar added. 1 cup of cream is an improvement.

CLAM CHOWDER.—*Mrs. W. F. C. Hasson.*

In the kettle in which the chowder is to be made fry several slices of salt pork. When nice and brown remove, and in the gravy put 4 large potatoes and 4 onions which have been chopped; season with salt and pepper, add from 1 quart to 3 pints of water, and boil half an hour. Take 1 quart of clams or 1 can, and after cutting off the black heads, chop and put them with the broth into the kettle about 10 minutes before taking up. When ready to serve, add pilot bread broken in small pieces.

CREAM OF CORN SOUP.—*Mrs. W. F. Jones.*

Remove the corn from 1 can; cover with 3 cups of water; simmer for one hour; press through a sieve. Scald 3 cups of milk: add the corn and 1 tablespoon of butter well mixed with 1 tablespoon of flour. Cook until smooth, season with salt and pepper, add $\frac{1}{2}$ cup of cream and stir until heated. Take from the fire, add 1 beaten egg, and serve at once. The egg or cream may be omitted, but the soup is far more delicious with the addition of both. The corn from twelve ears equals one can.

The Best

SUGAR CURED, HICKORY SMOKED

The most delicate] in flavor, and most economical in cut . . . . Ask your grocer for them . . .

Dodge, Sweeney & Co.   Distributing Agents

Orders Promptly Attended To.   Telephone Red 15

MARIN CENTRAL ~ BAKERY ~
and .... Confectionery

Genuine Milk and Rye **BREAD, and FANCY CAKES**

F. RIEDE, Proprietor

near Petaluma ave.   **FOURTH ST.** San Rafael.

S. HERZOG & CO.

M. Blumenthal
S. Herzog

Dealers in all kinds of

✂ Fresh and Salt Meats ✂

wholesale and retail

BEEF, VEAL, LAMB, MUTTON, HAM, ✂ BACON, ✂ TONGUES, SMOKED BEEF

All Kinds of Vegetables

NEW SAN RAFAEL MARKET
B STREET, Near 4th.

Fish and Shell Fish.

BOILED FISH.—*Mrs. L. A. Lancel.*
(To be served cold.)

Put into the fish kettle enough water to cover the fish; add 1 large onion, small piece of garlic, 1 dozen cloves, 1 dozen allspice, 4 laurel leaves, 2 carrots, celery, ½ cup of vinegar; cover tight, and boil ½ hour. Have the fish ready. Any fish of from 4 to 5 pounds will take from 15 to 20 minutes. When done, serve cold.

SAUCE FOR SAME.—Make a mayonnaise; add a small piece of garlic; let it stand about one hour. Chop cucumbers fine. When ready to serve, add pepper, salt, juice of lemon, and lastly the chopped cucumbers. If necessary, thin with cream.

TARTAR SAUCE FOR BROILED FISH.—*Mrs. R. E. Neil.*

2 tablespoons of mayonnaise, 2 tablespoons chopped capers, ½ onion grated. Mix 1 hour before using.

DRESSING FOR BOILED FISH.—*Mrs. R. E. Neil.*

6 raw tomatoes or ½ can; strain through a colander; add 3 tablespoons chopped capers, 1 large pickled cucumber, and 1 pickled onion chopped very fine with the capers, 4 tablespoons tomato catsup, a dash of cayenne, 1 teaspoon of salt, and 1 cup of stock. Simmer 10 minutes, and pour over boiled fish.

TURBOT A LA CREME.—*Mrs. E. R. Donohoe.*

Put ¼ pound of flour in a saucepan, mix it gently with 1 quart of milk, and be careful that it is not lumpy; then tie up together 2 small onions, a bunch of parsley or sprig of thyme, for if put in loose they will discolor the sauce, which must be white; add a little grated nutmeg, 1 teaspoonful of salt, ¼ teaspoonful of pepper; place it on a sharp fire, and stir it all the time; boil it until it forms a thickish paste: take it off the fire and add ½ pound of butter rather fresh, 2 yolks of eggs; mix them well into the sauce, and pass through a sieve; pour some of it into a dish which must be well buttered, then a layer of fresh codfish which should be already boiled and pulled to pieces to form small flakes; season it highly with pepper and salt, add more sauce, then the fish until it is all mixed up; sprinkle the top with bread crumbs and grated Parmesan cheese. Put it into a moderate oven for ½ hour, to give it a light brown color.

FISH AND SHELL FISH.

HOW TO PREPARE TERRAPIN.—*Mrs. A. W. Foster.*

Throw live terrapin into boiling water; after boiling fifteen minutes remove and take off black outside skin from the shell, the skin and nails from the claws; replace them in water a little salted, and cook until under shell cracks or feels soft to the touch. Remove the under shell carefully over a bowl, take out the sand-bag, remove head, gall-bag from the liver, and meat from upper shell.

TERRAPIN A LA BALTIMORE.—*Mrs. A. W. Foster.*

Place the meat, cloves, and eggs if any, of two terrapin in a saucepan; add a dash of cayenne, white pepper, a grating of nutmeg. small saltspoon of ground cloves, a wine glass of Madeira or sherry. Cook five minutes and put away to cool for future use. Place in a saucepan a cup of good stock, add a glass of Madeira. Blend ½ cup of butter with 2 tablespoons of flour; add this to the gravy, with a piece of lemon. Put in the terrapin, and heat. Have ready the yolks of 6 hard boiled eggs mashed fine; beat and mix gradually with the terrapin. The whites of the eggs can be chopped fine and added.

Terrapin a la Maryland differs only in substituting cream for stock. The cream is warmed and added gradually to the eggs at the las minute, and not allowed to boil. Epicures prefer stock to cream.

TERRAPIN STEW.—*Mrs. W. B. Bradford.*

Boil according to size 30 or 40 minutes, so that the upper shell will separate from the lower easily. Take gall-bag from liver, which is always found on the right lobe; avoid breaking, as it would give a bitter taste and spoil the dish. Strip the skin from the claws, cut off the nails and skin the head. Throw nothing away but the gall-bag. Cut all in small pieces and stew all slowly in sherry wine, with a good supply or butter and red pepper, for 1½ hours, keeping closely covered all the time. Salt to taste. If they have no eggs in them, add two hard boiled hens' eggs to each terrapin just before the stew is done. Add a little flour rubbed in butter, just before taking from the fire. Place crispy toast on platter. Serve with baked potatoes and celery.

SARDINES AND ANCHOVY SAUCE.—*Mrs. Geo. Boyd.*

Put piece of butter size of an egg into saucepan; when melted, stir in the yolks of 2 eggs, a salt spoon cayenne, and 2 tablespoons anchovy sauce. Add a tablespoon of weak sherry (don't cook on a hot fire). Pour this sauce over the sardines which have been laid on toast with sardine oil poured over them, and thoroughly heated in oven.

DEVILED CLAMS, NO. 1.—*Mrs. A. A. Smith.*

Chop fine 25 clams; cook for 20 minutes in a double boiler; drain and save the liquor. Rub 2 tablespoons of flour and 1 of butter together, and add to the liquor; when boiling, add the beaten yolks of two eggs, a dash of red pepper, a tablespoon each of chopped onions and parsley, and the clams. Mix and fill into shells; dust with crumbs, and brown in a quick oven.

FISH AND SHELL FISH.

DEVILED CLAMS, NO. 2.—*Mrs. A. A. Smith.*

Chop 50 clams very fine; take 2 tomatoes and 1 onion chopper equally fine, a little parsley, thyme and sweet marjoram, a little salt and pepper, and ½ cup of bread crumbs; add the juice of the clams till it is of the consistency of sausage; put in shells with lump of butter on each; cover with bread crumbs and bake ½ hour.

ESCALOPED CLAMS.—*Mrs. W. F. C. Hasson.*

Wash clean 100 clams; use only the soft part and the string part chopped fine; put a layer in the bottom of a buttered baking dish season with salt, pepper, cayenne and a little mace; sprinkle on plenty of stale bread crumbs and a quantity of bits of butter; repeat the layer until the dish is full; put plenty of butter on top, and pour in a cup of the water from the clams; bake in a moderate oven for one hour, and when half done, pour in a good glass of sherry.

CLAM CHOWDER.—*Mrs. W. F. Jones.*

Fry ½ pound of salt pork cut in small bits and 1 large sliced onion together, until brown. Chop the necks of the clams, and add to the mixture, also the clams and juice, and 3 or 4 potatoes cut like dice; let all simmer together about ½ hour. Season with salt and pepper, and thicken with a teaspoon of corn starch. This is too thick to serve as soup but takes the place of a fish course. If one prefers this in soup add 1 quart of milk, and serve as such.

OYSTERS AND MUSHROOMS.—*Dr. C. B. Brown, S. F.*

1 tablespoon butter and 1 tablespoon of flour cooked together; add ½ cup of mushroom liquor; when thick, add 1 quart oysters and 1 cup of mushrooms, 2 eggs beaten light, 1 teaspoon salt, and a dash of cayenne.

OYSTER COCKTAIL.—*Mrs. Carter P. Pomeroy.*

100 California oysters, 3 tablespoons of unsweetened tomato catsup, 4 tablespoons oyster liquor, 1 tablespoon Worcestershire sauce, juice of 1 large lemon, 1 dash of tobasco, salt to taste; mix well, and place on ice 1 hour.

CREAMED OYSTERS.—*Mrs. W. F. Jones.*

Melt a lump of butter the size of an egg in a sauce pan. Stir into it a heaping tablespoon of flour. Let this cook but not brown, and then add 1 large cup of rich cream previously warmed, a dash of cayenne, about 1 level teaspoon of salt, and a little Worcestershire sauce. This is for 3 dozen large oysters. When smooth, skim the oysters from the pan in which they have been heating, and add to the cream. Let them puff up, and when the edges curl they are done. Add a little of the oyster juice to thin the mixture, according to judgment and taste.

TOASTED ANGELS.—*Mrs. W. F. C. Hasson.*

Wrap a large oyster in a very thin slice of bacon or fat salt pork, putting on the oyster a little cayenne and 2 drops of lime juice; fasten with a string, or pin the bacon with a wooden toothpick; broil till the bacon is crisp, and serve very hot on squares of buttered toast.

OYSTERS COOKED WITH RICE.—*Mrs. W. F. Jones.*

Wash carefully 2 cups of rice and put it on to cook with the strained juice from a quart of fresh oysters, salt, and enough water to cook it until tender. When tender add ½ cup of butter and the beaten yolks of two eggs. Remove from the fire, and when a little cool stir in the well-beaten whites; turn into a buttered baking dish, smooth over the top. and then with the back of a spoon make dents deep enough to hold an oyster; then close together. Sprinkle with salt, pepper, ½ cup cracker crumbs, and small pieces of butter added last. Brown in oven quickly. Canned oysters can be used.

FANCY ROAST OYSTERS.—*Mrs. Sidney Cushing.*

Put 1 tablespoon of butter in saucepan, add ½ saltspoon white pepper, 1 teaspoon salt, a little cayenne, 2 tablespoons tomato catsup. When hot, add 1 pint of oysters, and cook until plump and the edges curl; serve on toast. Can be cooked in chafing dish.

SHRIMPS ON TOAST.—*Mrs. W. F. Jones.*

1 cup of rich cream to 1 pound of picked shrimps; salt, and a dash of cayenne. Cook all together and serve on buttered toast. A few drops of Worcestershire is an improvement.

SHRIMPS AND TOMATOES.—*Mrs. McMahon.*

1 large tablespoon butter and 1 tablespoon flour, browned together. Scrape in a little onion, 3 or 4 cloves, and a few drops of Worcestershire sauce. To this add a can of tomatoes strained, or an equal amount of fresh cooked ones, 1 pound of picked shrimps, a small wine glass of white wine, add a teacup of sweet cream with a pinch of soda in it. Cook all together 20 minutes.

CREAMED CRAB OR SHRIMPS.—*Mrs. W. F. Jones.*

1 large picked crab or 1 pint of picked shrimps, 1 cup of cream, ½ cup of milk, 1 heaping tablespoon flour, 1 teaspoon salt, dash of cayenne, 1 tablespoon butter, and a few drops of Worcestershire if desirable. Put the cream on the stove with the crab or shrimps in it. Stir the flour into the milk and add when the cream is hot; then the other ingredients, and when well cooked put into seven individual shells; roll one cracker to dust over the top, and put some butter in center. Bake until brown. The shells can be filled the day before they are baked, if kept in a cool place.

STEWED CRAB.—*Mrs. Geo. Boyd.*

Take 6 cups water; a bouquet composed of 1 sprig thyme, 1 sprig celery, a little parsley, and 1 bay leaf; a little whole mace, 1 onion chopped fine, a lemon sliced, and 1 green pepper; boil at least 1 hour. Strain; add 2 raw eggs well beaten, let it boil; then put in half a pound of butter creamed, and enough flour for thickening, a tablespoon of powdered mace, some chopped parsley, and cayenne pepper to taste.

Have the crabs boiled half an hour; cut in pieces, leaving the shells on excepting the back, saving the water which must be added to the gravy. Put in the crabs and cook for half an hour in a double kettle. This is nice also for soft shell crabs.

DEVILED CRAB.—*Mrs. Oge.*

Clean and shred a crab; add to it 3 tablespoons melted butter, ½ cup of clear soup stock, salt, a little red and black pepper, the crumbs from the inside of a milk loaf, using no crust, and 3 tablespoons of thick, sweet cream. Put all in shells and bake until a light brown, for about 20 minutes.

CRAB CHOPS.—*Mrs. W. F. Jones.*

Boil 2 crabs and pick in small pieces. Melt one tablespoon of butter and stir into it 1 tablespoon of flour; when well mixed, add 1 cup of hot water. This gravy must be good and thick. Stir in the crab, add 1 beaten egg, ½ a lemon, a dash of cayenne, and salt to taste. Place it on a board in the form of a square and about ¾ of an inch thick. Put in a cool place or leave until next day; then divide your square into smaller squares, and cut each small square into two pieces from corner to corner; each piece should be about the size of a small lamb chop. Roll in egg and cracker crumbs, and fry in hot fat. Place around the edge of platter, and in the pointed end of each piece insert the sharp claw of the crab, leaving the large end showing to look like a chop bone.

SAUCE FOR SAME.—Cook 1 quart of tomatoes until thick, season with butter, salt, and a dash of cayenne. Pour in the center of platter.

CRAB FRICASSEE.—*Mrs. Jas. Oliver,*

1 crab, ¼ pint milk, ½ tablespoon mustard, piece butter, season with salt and pepper; mix well, and let it come to a boil. Then stir in crab and beaten yolk of an egg. Put into a dish sprinkled with cracker crumbs and bits of butter.

CRAB CREOLE.—*Mrs. Sidney Cushing.*
(Chafing dish.)

Rub a stewpan with a piece of garlic; then put in 2 ounces of butter, 3 green onions, and 2 green peppers chopped fine; add salt, pepper, and cayenne, and stew slowly 10 minutes. Then add 1 large tomato without the skin, cut in small pieces; stew this until the tomato is dissolved; also add a teaspoon of flour and good cream enough to make thick as drawn-butter; add a picked crab, and serve on buttered toast.

CRAB STEW.—*Mrs. W. F. Jones.*

Pick one crab to pieces, and add 1 cup of milk, a dash of cayenne, salt, and a heaping teaspoon of flour stirred into a little cold milk; also 1 tablespoon butter and 2 eggs. Pour into the center of a platter, and make a border of 1 cup of boiled rice that has been cooked in milk to which a good spoonful of butter was added.

LOBSTER CUTLETS.—*Mrs. W. B. Noble.*

Boil 1 large lobster for 30 minutes; remove the meat, and chop it rather fine. Put a half pint of milk on to boil. Rub together 1 large tablespoon of butter, and 3 rounding tablespoons of flour, and stir into the milk when boiling; stir, and cook until this forms a thick paste, then add the slightly beaten yolks of two eggs; take from the fire, and add 2 cups of the chopped lobster, a tablespoon of chopped parsley, ½ teaspoon of onion juice, ¼ of a nutmeg grated, ¼ teaspoon of white pepper, and a palatable seasoning of salt and cayenne; mix, and turn out to cool. When cold form into chops about the size and shape of a French mutton chop; dip first in beaten egg, and then in bread crumbs, and fry in smoking hot fat. When done, drain on brown paper; stick a claw of the lobster in the end of the chop to represent the mutton bone.

LOBSTER A LA NEWBERG.—*Mrs. E. W. Newhall.*

Cut the best part of a lobster into small pieces. Rub the creamy fat through a sieve, and stir into this 1 teaspoon of butter blended with 2 teaspoons of flour. Put into a hot dish 1 tablespoon of butter; when it creams, season with salt, pepper, and a speck of cayenne, and add ½ cup of sherry; pour this over the well-beaten yolks of 2 eggs; return to fire, and add gradually 1 cup of cream; pour this over the creamy fat, and cook a few minutes; add the pieces of lobster which must be seasoned with salt, pepper, and a squeeze of lemon juice; and cook 10 minutes.

LOBSTER A LA MARYLAND.—*Dr. C. B. Brown, S. F.*

To a pint of cream just at the boiling point add 4 lobsters (or crawfish) cut in small pieces and seasoned with salt, pepper, and a pinch of red pepper. Add the well-beaten yolks of 4 eggs, 1 tablespoon of flour mixed with water to a paste, and a large wine glass of sherry. Serve very hot. This is a fine chafing dish recipe.

GARNISH FOR FISH.—*Mrs. W. F. Jones.*

Cut lemons in halves, and remove all the pulp and juice. Whip butter to a cream, add lemon juice (not enough to curdle the butter), a little chopped parsley and a dash of cayenne. Place around your platter, alternating with sprigs of parsley.

D. W. Martens & Co.

San Rafael, . . Cal.

Grocers

Teas, Coffees, and Spices a Specialty.

Grain, Produce, Vegetables, Fresh Fish and Oysters . . .

Fourth St., cor. D.

Foreign and Domestic Fruits.

TELEPHONE NO. 82.

W. H. Anderson

GENERAL MARKETING

and . . Fine Groceries.

COR. B AND THIRD STREET,   San Rafael.

J. Kelly . . .

Orders promptly Attended to.

Wholesale and Retail Dealer in

MARIN CO. MARKET AND MILLER BLOCK.

Fruits and Vegetables

Fourth St. bet. A and B.

TELEPHONE BLACK 51.   **SAN RAFAEL.**

Meats, Poultry, Game
and Meats Rechauffe.

Rules for Cooking Meats.

Put all salt meats to cook in cold water; all fresh meats, excepting for soups, into hot water, then cook slowly.

All roast meats, excepting veal, are put dry into a very hot oven; veal requiring a little more moisture. When well browned, add hot water; and when about half done, salt. Never salt meat until partially cooked.

Rare meat requires about 15 minutes to the pound.

Baste all roasts frequently.

Roast beef requires a hotter oven than any other meat.

YORKSHIRE PUDDING.—*Mrs. W. F. Jones.*

To be eaten with roast beef. 1 cup of flour, 1 egg, 1 cup of milk, 1 teaspoon of salt. Have the pan quite hot in which is some of the roast dripping; pour in the pudding, and bake in a quick oven. This is preferable to the old way of raising the roast and baking the pudding underneath.

FILLET OF BEEF A LA ROSSINI.—*Mrs. W. F. C. Hasson.*

Braise a larded fillet with what vegetables are in season; moisten while cooking, with a bottle of good claret, some say sherry. When done, glaze and dish it up garnished with macaroni prepared as follows: Boil ½ pound of macaroni cut in 3 inch lengths; put in a stew pan with some sliced mushrooms, ½ pint good stock, 3 ounces grated Parmesan cheese, and a pat of butter; season with salt and pepper; toss over the fire till well mixed, and serve around the beef. Pour over the beef the gravy from the pan, with the vegetables strained out.

FILLET OF BEEF WITH MUSHROOM SAUCE.
—*Mrs. J. E. Alexander.*

The fillet is the tenderloin of beef. Have the butcher prepare and lard it with strips of salt pork ready for the oven; pepper, and spread thickly with butter; add a little salt to ¼ cup boiling water, and pour into the pan. Bake in a quick oven 30 or 40 minutes, basting 4 or 5 times.

MUSHROOM SAUCE.—1 can of French mushrooms, 1 cup of stock, 1 cup of cream, 2 tablespoons flour, 2 tablespoons butter; salt and pepper to taste. Melt the butter, add the flour, stir until a dark brown, then gradually add the stock; when this boils up, add the liquor from the mushrooms; season and simmer 20 minutes; add the mushrooms and let cook 5 minutes more, then add the cream; let it boil up and remove immediately. Pour it around the fillet and serve.

BEEFSTEAK AND MUSHROOMS.—*Mrs. J. E. Alexander.*

Put into a saucepan 1 ounce of butter, a small onion chopped fine, a little ground sage and thyme, and place over the fire. When hot, shake in 2 tablespoons flour, and when it becomes brown, put in 1 gill of water and let it boil for ½ hour; then add 3 tablespoons of beef stock, a little suet and a little nutmeg. Put in 1 can of mushrooms; let it boil for 10 minutes; and pour over a nicely broiled beefsteak.

BEEFSTEAK ROLL.—*Mrs. W. F. Jones.*

Take a slice of round steak, not too thick, and spread it with a dressing made of 1 cup of bread crumbs, 1 small onion chopped fine, 1 tablespoon of butter, seasoned with salt, pepper, and sage. Wet with a little cold water. Roll up the steak and tie securely. especially at the ends. Fry a couple of slices of salt pork in a pan, and in this brown the roll thoroughly. Pour hot water over it, cover tightly, and cook slowly for 2 hours. Then add thickening and seasoning. This is not so dry as when baked. Heart is also better cooked this way than baked. Cook the onion in a little butter and water before putting it into the dressing.

PIGS IN BLANKETS.—*Mrs. A. A. Smith.*

Cut a round steak into 4-inch squares; place on each square a thin slice of bacon, a clove, and a small bay leaf; add pepper and salt; roll up and skewer; put some butter in the bottom of a stewpan with a little minced onion; place the pigs in this, and fry brown; then add just enough water to stew; keep adding boiling water as it is needed, having enough gravy at the last to thicken and pour over them.

CURRY.—*A. E. Menzies.*

Brown onion and apple; for a good dish of meat take 2 onions and 3 or 4 apples. Chop the apple, slice the onion; take these out of frying pan, after being browned, and if fresh meat is used, brown it. Take 1 tablespoon of flour, 1 dessertspoon of curry powder; mix smoothly with milk; add to the rest of the ingredients with a large cup of milk. Stew in a saucepan for 2 hours, cooking very slowly, stirring now and then. A few cold string beans, or peas that have been cooked, are an improvement; also a little sweet pickle.

PEPPER STEW.—*Mrs. Herbert Kellogg.*

Put 3 onions into beef dripping, and cook moderately until soft, being careful not to scorch them. Add 1 pound of raw beef cut into small pieces, 3 red peppers, first removing all the veins and seeds; or if preferred, bell peppers can be used. ½ hour before serving, add ½ can of corn or 4 ears scraped from the cob, and 3 or 4 fresh peeled tomatoes. Season with salt and pour over toast. It should cook slowly for at least 1½ hours.

KIDNEY STEW.—*Mrs. W. B. Bradford.*

2 beeves' kidneys cut up very fine; pour hot water over, and as it

boils, pour off and add fresh water; then let it simmer slowly for 2 hours. Cut up 2 large onions, add to the stew, and cook 1 hour. About 2 minutes before serving add a little curry, thicken with flour, add wine, and serve on toast.

KIDNEY STEW.—*Mrs. P. T. Burtchaell.*

Parboil the kidneys and pour off the water. Have frying-pan hot, put in a piece of butter, and fry 1 onion in same until brown; drain kidneys, put in frying-pan with onion and fry brown. Put saucepan on with a wineglass of sherry, let boil 1 minute, then turn kidneys in with salt, pepper, ½ teaspoon of allspice and cinnamon; add water to cover; thicken with a little flour. Mushrooms may be added if desired.

VEAL CUTLETS.—*Mrs. W. F. Jones.*

Lay the cutlets on a board and chop on both sides until they are quite ragged; roll in egg and cracker crumbs; put into a pan where there is plenty of hot fat, and cook rather slowly for 20 minutes, or until they are a nice brown; salt them and place on a platter. Put 1 tablespoon of flour into fat remaining in the pan, and let cook a few minutes, stirring constantly; then gradually add milk until the gravy is of the right consistency. Season, and pour over cutlets, or serve separately.

VEAL LOAF, STEAMED.—*Mrs Carter P. Pomeroy.*

2 pounds of veal and ¼ pound of salt pork, put through sausage grinder; 2 cups of bread crumbs soaked in stock or milk; 2 eggs unbeaten; a little grated onion; salt and pepper; steam in pudding pail 2 hours. This is good served hot in slices with tomato sauce: or cold with mayonnaise dressing; or for a cold lunch dish; very easily made, and sure to be good.

VEAL CROQUETTES.—*Mrs. Wm. B. Noble.*

Put ½ pound of bread to soak in 1 pint of cold water; ½ pound of cold veal to be chopped fine. Press the bread through a cloth to extract all the water. Put into a stew pan 2 ounces of butter and 1 tablespoon of onion chopped very fine; fry for 2 minutes; add the bread and stir until rather dry. Then add the meat, a little grated nutmeg and lemon peel, with salt and pepper to taste. Stir continually until very hot, then add 2 eggs, one at a time; mix well together, then spread on a dish to cool. Make into egg-shaped balls, dip into egg and bread-crumb them, then fry in boiling fat to a light brown.

CHICKEN CROQUETTES.—*Mrs. Wm. B. Noble.*

Remove the skin, fat and bones from one cold boiled chicken; then chop, or grind, as for mince meat. Take 2 tablespoons of butter into which work 1 large tablespoon of flour; to this add ½ pint of cream or rich milk, ¼ of a nutmeg grated, a pinch of ground mace, 1 teaspoon of scraped onion, 1 tablespoon of chopped parsley, with salt and pepper to taste. Place this mixture, with the chicken, in a pan, and stew it about 5 minutes; remove from the fire and add the yolks of 2 eggs; mix thoroughly and spread on a dish to cool. When cold, take about 1 teaspoonful and roll in flour, and shape in a mold or a wineglass. Then take the yolks of 2 eggs, 1 tablespoon of cream, 1 teaspoon of lemon juice, and a little salt; mix well, dip the croquettes first in this and then in fine bread crumbs. Fry in boiling fat, a light brown. These may be warmed over by putting them in a warm oven, not too hot or they will dry.

PRESSED CHICKEN OR VEAL.—*Mrs. W. F. Jones.*

Cut up a full grown chicken, or 2 pounds of veal stew; put to cook in a small amount of water, cover tightly and cook 4 or 5 hours. Pour off the liquid and strain into another saucepan; there should be a good cupful of rich juice. Remove all bones and the skin of the chicken; pull the meat apart, put it into the juice and return to the fire. Season highly with salt and pepper, pour into bread pan, and set away to get cold. A few slices of cooked carrots cut in fancy shapes and placed in the bottom of the pan before pouring in the meat, improve the appearance. Garnish with parsley. Nice for lunch or an entree.

CHICKEN TERRAPIN.—*Mrs. J. E. Alexander*
(For a chafing dish.)

Cut a cold chicken into small pieces, removing all bone and gristle. Put into the chafing dish ½ pint of cream and ¼ pound of butter rubbed into a large spoonful of flour; pepper and salt to taste. Add the chicken, and when it boils up, add 3 hard boiled eggs chopped fine, and the juice of a lemon. Simmer for a moment and serve.

FRICASSEE CHICKEN.—*Mrs. E. B. Mahon.*

Split the chickens down the back, dry and dredge with flour; add pepper and salt: put in a pan with some bits of butter, cover with 1 quart of water: put in oven, and closely cover with another pan which may be removed when the chickens are nearly done, to let them brown; thicken the gravy: serve with mashed potatoes.

CHICKEN AU SUPREME.—*Dr. C. B. Brown, S. F.*

1 tablespoon butter, 1 tablespoon flour rubbed together, ½ pint of milk; cook until thick; add ½ teaspoon onion juice. Cut into dice 2 cups of cooked chicken or turkey which have stood from ½ hour to 2 hours in 2 tablespoons olive oil: add ½ teaspoon celery salt, ½ teaspoon white salt, and a dash of cayenne.

SEVERAL WAYS TO COOK CHICKEN.—*Mrs. W. F. Jones.*

Take young chickens to fry; or if old they must be steamed first, then jointed, rubbed dry, rolled in flour, and fried in butter; or equal quantities of butter and dripping can be used. There must be plenty of fat; and after the chicken is well browned on both sides, add salt, cover tightly, and remove to where it will cook slowly, for at least ½ hour; turn occasionally. Put 1 heaping tablespoon of flour in fat; after the chicken is done, pour in milk to the right consistency; season, and pour over chicken, or serve in gravy boat.

WHITE FRICASSEE.—Joint the chickens and put to cook in hot water, pouring on water about ½ the depth of chicken. Cover tightly, and cook slowly from 2 to 5 hours, according to age of chicken. ½ hour before serving, season, make a drawn butter gravy of the broth, and let the chicken simmer in this on back of stove. Serve on split biscuit or toast, or place boiled rice around the edge of the platter. Some prefer a cream gravy.

SMOTHERED CHICKEN.—Split down the back young chickens ¾ grown; spread with butter, cover with another pan, and bake ½ hour. Season and brown before serving. Some brown the chicken on the broiler.

CHICKEN SOUFFLE.—*Mrs. W. F. C. Hasson.*

1 pint chopped chicken, 1 tablespoon butter, 1 tablespoon chopped parsley, 1 pint of milk, 2 dashes of pepper, 1 tablespoon flour, 3 eggs, and ½ cup of stale bread crumbs; put the butter into a small saucepan, and when melted add the flour and mix till smooth. Then add the milk and stir continually until it boils, add the crumbs, cook 1 minute; take from the fire, add salt, pepper, parsley, chicken, and the yolks of the eggs well beaten. Beat the whites to a stiff froth, stir them into the mixture carefully. Pour into a well greased baking dish, and bake in a quick oven for 20 minutes. Serve immediately or it will fall.

CREAMED CHICKEN.—*Mrs. J. E. Alexander.*

1 chicken, 4 sweetbreads, 1 can mushrooms. Boil sweetbreads ½ hour, chicken until tender. When cold, cut up as for salad. In a saucepan put 4 large tablespoons of butter; when melted, stir in 5 tablespoons of flour, add 1 quart of rich milk, or ½ cream and ½ milk; stir until it thickens; flavor with a little onion juice, black and red pepper, and a little nutmeg. Put all together in a baking dish and cover with bread crumbs; add a little of the chicken broth. Bake 20 minutes. Oysters, mushrooms and sweetbreads are delicious prepared in the same way.

KEYSTONE PATES.—*Mrs. W. B. Noble.*

Chop cold cooked meat fine, measure, and to every pint add 1 tablespoon of butter, 2 tablespoons of dried bread crumbs, ½ cup of stock or boiling water, 2 eggs slightly beaten, and salt and pepper to taste. Put all these ingredients into a saucepan, and stir over the fire for a moment until thoroughly mixed. Fill custard cups ⅔ full with this mixture, stand them in a baking pan ½ full of boiling water, and bake in a moderate oven 20 minutes. When done, turn them out carefully on a heated dish, and pour around them Bechamel sauce. Remains of any cold meat or poultry are delightful used in this way.

SCRAPPLE.—*Mrs. T. Stratton.*

Boil 2 pounds of beef or pork in enough water to cover it well, until the bones can be easily removed; take out the meat and chop it fine; skim the fat from the water, and when it comes to a boil again, stir in the chopped meat; add sage, salt and pepper to taste; stir into this enough corn meal to make it thick as mush; add the fat, or a part of it as desired; stir for 5 or 10 minutes; pour into a pan, and when cold cut

MEATS, POULTRY AND GAME.

into slices and fry brown quickly. This is nice for breakfast or luncheon, and will keep a week in a cool place.

BACON AND RICE.—*Mrs. W. B. Bradford.*

Boil 2 pounds of bacon until tender. Boil 2 cups of rice, to which add while cooking ½ cup of raisins not chopped. Put the bacon in the center of a platter, and over the rice sprinkle almonds chopped and blanched. 1 pound of nuts before they are shelled will be about right. Nice for an entree.

DEVILED CHOPS.—*Mrs. W. F. C. Hasson.*

Mix well together 1 ounce butter, 1 teaspoon made mustard, ½ teaspoon French mustard, salt, pepper, cayenne, 1 teaspoon hot Chutney, 1 teaspoon grated horse-radish, a little Chili vinegar, and the juice of 1 lime. Rub a little of this on 2 thick mutton chops broiled rare, and put the rest of the sauce over them in a very hot dish.

PORK PIE.—*Mrs. V. Neale.*

(To be served cold with breakfast or lunch.)

Cut up some cold roast pork into rather large dice; have ⅔ meat and ⅓ fat; put the bones and trimmings in a saucepan, and make a good gravy out of them. Put the pork into a deep pie dish, season well with salt, pepper, a little sage, and a very little chopped onion. Fill halfway with part of the gravy (cooled and seasoned), cover with a good plain short crust, ornament with paste leaves, and bake about ¾ of an hour in a moderate oven until brown; then take it out and pour the remainder of the gravy (hot) through the hole in the center until nearly full. Memorandum: Be sure to make a small hole in center before placing the pie in the oven, otherwise it will not be wholesome. When cold the gravy should be all in a jelly; and the whole should be well seasoned.

PORK AND BEANS.—*Mrs. C. F. Robinson.*

Put 1 pint of pea beans in bean pot, with 1 tablespoon of syrup, a dash of cayenne, and 1 pound of fat salt pork, scored, placed on top; cover with cold water, and bake in moderate oven from 12 to 24 hours, adding hot water as it evaporates. They must not be allowed to get dry until the last hour, when the water must be somewhat cooked down. If these directions are followed, the beans need not be soaked over night.

HAM, SUGAR BAKED.—*Miss Parsons, Tamalpais.*

Put the ham to soak in cold water the morning of the day before cooking. Put it over the fire next day, and boil 6 or 7 hours, until soft, or until a fork can be turned partly around in the rind. Strip off the rind, which can be done readily if the ham is done enough. Rub over the surface ½ cup of brown sugar; put into the oven in a dripping pan, and bake until nicely browned, or about an hour in a slow oven. In serving, slice very thin.

TO BAKE A HAM.—*Mrs. W. F. Jones.*

Soak a ham over night; in the morning scrape, clean, and cover the ham all over with a paste about ½ inch thick made of graham flour wet in cold water; as the ham bakes, fill the cracks which form with some reserved paste. Put it into the pan dry and bake about 5 hours in a slow oven, or longer if the ham is very large. Remove crust, skin and all, and stick the ham with cloves; rub with bread crumbs, and brown, or frost, and garnish the bone with fancy paper.

TO BOIL HAM.—*Mrs. L. A. Lancel.*

Wash the ham thoroughly, and soak it if necessary. Have boiling ½ gallon of claret with enough water to cover the ham; a good-sized ham will need to boil 3 hours, or until a fork enters easily. When done, remove the skin; sprinkle the ham with bread crumbs on top, and stick in a few cloves; then brown in the oven. Or, if boiled in water, when the skin is removed, while hot pour over it champagne or brandy with a little sugar; keep on pouring till about 1 cupful is absorbed, letting the ham remain in the liquid until cold.

STEWED FRESH TONGUE.—*Mrs. W. F. C. Hasson.*

Soak a fresh tongue in cold water 1 hour; boil 3 hours, and put on one side till cold. Put it in a stewpan, cover with stock, add salt, cayenne, 1 dozen cloves, 1 turnip, 1 carrot, 2 onions, and ½ head celery, all cut very small. Stew gently 1½ hours; take out the tongue and add to the gravy 1 tablespoon made mustard, 3 tablespoons mushroom catsup, 1 tablespoon Worcestershire, 3 pickled gherkins chopped fine, 1 tumbler port or red wine, and 2 ounces butter braided with 3 tablespoons browned flour; boil and stir this till smooth; put back the tongue and simmer ½ an hour; dish the tongue, and pour the sauce over it.

SHEEP'S TONGUE, SPANISH.—*Miss H. Pregge.*

Put 8 sheep's tongues into water and boil until tender; skin while hot, then slice them and place in a saucepan with 1 can of tomatoes; add a little onion, pepper, and salt. Boil ½ hour; before removing from the stove, thicken with 1 tablespoon of flour.

BOILED LAMBS' TONGUES.—*Mrs L. A. Lancel.*

Take as many lambs' tongues as you like, clean and put in boiling water; add salt, pepper, celery, carrots, turnips, laurel leaves, a little green pepper, and garlic. Boil all together till done; peel, and serve very hot. Boiled calves' feet, same as lambs' tongues.

SAUCE FOR LAMBS' TONGUES OR CALVES' FEET.—Take small chives, eschalots, and parsley; chop fine. Mix well 2 heaping tablespoons of the chopped greens, 6 tablespoons of olive oil, 8 of vinegar, ½ tablespoon of salt, ½ teaspoon of pepper, ½ cup capers; serve on hot tongue.

CALVES' FEET A LA MARECHAL.—*Mrs. W. F. C. Hasson.*

Boil, bone and cut into inch pieces, 4 calves' feet. Fry till soft in 4 ounces butter, 2 onions, a little garlic, 2 green peppers and some mushrooms, all chopped small; add salt, pepper, cayenne, and a little mace; stir in 4 tablespoons of flour, and then add boiling milk enough to make the mixture as thick as rich cream. Put in the feet, and mix all well together. Take off the fire, add the yolks of 2 eggs, the juice of a lime, and a tablespoon of water, all well beaten together; pour this mixture into a buttered pan, and put it by until cold; cut into slices, dip twice into egg and bread crumb, fry to a light brown in butter, and serve very hot.

TRIPE, SPANISH.—*Miss H. Pregge.*

Take about 2 pounds of tripe (honey-comb is the best): wash thoroughly and cut into small pieces; then put into a saucepan and scald with boiling water for 10 or 15 minutes; pour off the water and add 1 quart of tomatoes, a little salt, a small piece of green or red pepper and about 5 whole cloves, a small onion cut fine, and a lime thinly sliced. Boil for 1 hour and thicken with 1 tablespoon of moistened flour; serve hot. To be nice, the tripe must be fresh and tender.

FROGS A LA POULETTE.—*Mrs. W. F. C. Hasson.*

Joint the hind legs and backs of 12 frogs; put in a closely covered stewpan with some truffles, a small can of mushrooms sliced, a glass of good white wine, salt, white pepper, cayenne, mace, and 4 ounces butter; stew gently 15 minutes, stirring once or twice; if then tender, add 1 teaspoon cornstarch rubbed into 1 ounce of butter; let it cook 2 minutes, take from the fire, and stir in the yolks of 6 eggs beat up well with ½ pint cream. Do not put on the fire again after putting in the eggs. Cut the inside of a German loaf into a nice shape and fry brown; put into the center of the dish, and stick into it skewers decorated with truffles, limes, and mushrooms. Put the frogs and sauce around this, and serve very hot.

CANVAS-BACK DUCKS.—*Mrs. W. F. Jones.*

Tie the skin tightly to the neck of the duck, then put inside 1 level tablespoon salt and 1 teacup of water. Sew up as tightly as possible, put in a dry pan and bake in a hot oven from 20 to 30 minutes, according to size of duck. As the ducks brown, turn them; when done serve immediately.

STEWED SQUABS.—*Mrs. W. F. C. Hasson.*

Make a stuffing of the livers and hearts chopped fine with a little butter, chopped pork, the yolk of an egg, salt, cayenne, and a little lemon. Stuff with this 6 squabs, put them in a stewpan, cover with stock, and stew gently ½ hour; take out the birds and add salt, cayenne. 3 tablespoons mushroom catsup, 1 tablespoon Worcestershire, 1 tablespoon lime juice, 1 large glass of port or sherry, and 2 ounces butter braided with 2 tablespoons browned flour; put back the birds for 10 minutes. Fry some thick slices of bread, stand a bird on each, and pour the sauce over all.

SWEETBREADS.—*Dr. C. B. Brown, S. F.*

Parboil 2 pairs or 1 pound of sweetbreads 15 minutes, blanch, and cut into dice. Melt 1 tablespoon of butter, add 1 rounded tablespoon of flour, and cook until thick; slowly add ½ pint of cream, and 1 gill asparagus liquor; cook together until the sauce is thick; add the sweetbreads, and 1 cup of fresh asparagus cut into small pieces. Stir carefully until cooked, adding 1 teaspoon salt and a dash of cayenne.

SWEETBREADS.—*Mrs. W. F. C. Hasson.*

Lay the sweetbreads in cold water for 12 hours, changing the water several times; then boil them 5 minutes, drop into cold water, skin them, and lard them with fat bacon. Put in a stewpan 1 small carrot, 2 small onions, and a teaspoon parsley all minced, the sweetbreads and 1 pint of stock; season with salt, pepper, cayenne, and a little mace, and stew till tender. Clean and slice a dozen mushrooms, boil them 5 minutes in water and lime juice, drain them, and put them in a stewpan with a pint of good brown sauce; stew till reduced $\frac{1}{2}$. Dish the sweetbreads, and pour the sauce over them.

QUAIL PATE.—*Mrs. I. A. Lancel.*

6 quail, or same amount of chicken, 2 pounds veal, 1 pound fresh pork. Put into a bean pot a layer of quail, pork and veal alternately: season each layer with pepper, salt, a little garlic, and a few bay leaves; keep on until all the meat is used; add $\frac{1}{2}$ pint of good stock: some use white wine. Cover tightly so that no steam can escape; mix a paste of flour and water to put around the cover so that the jar will be air-tight. Bake $2\frac{1}{4}$ hours in a moderate oven. The meat can also be chopped fine, and baked in the same way. The bones of the veal should be placed on top of the meat when ready to be covered for the oven.

BRAINS A LA VINAIGRETTE.—*Mrs. Walter S. Hobart.*

(Dinner entree after soup.)

Put into a frying-pan two large tablespoons butter; make smoking brown. Add 1 tablespoon chopped estregon or small garlic, 1 tablespoon chopped eschalot, 1 tablespoon of chopped parsley, 1 cup of bouillon or soup, 1 cup of white wine, 2 tablespoons of vinegar, 3 or 4 bay leaves, black pepper and salt to taste. Boil all together 10 minutes; add prepared brains to the mixture, and boil 15 minutes. Let the brains be divided in large pieces, not chopped fine.

HAGGIS.—*Mrs. Wm. B. Noble.*

Chop the uncooked heart, tongue, and half of the liver of a sheep, and mix with them a little less than half their weight in chopped bacon; add $\frac{1}{2}$ cup of stale bread crumbs, the grated rind of 1 lemon, 1 teaspoon of salt, $\frac{1}{4}$ teaspoon of white pepper, and 2 well beaten eggs; pack this into a buttered mold, cover, place it in a kettle partly filled with boiling water, and boil slowly for 2 hours. When done turn it on a dish, and serve it plain or with sauce Bechamel. This is a famous Scotch dish, and when once tried will be repeated.

SAUCE BECHAMEL.—*Mrs. Wm. B. Noble.*

Put 1 tablespoon of butter in a frying-pan; when melted add an even tablespoon of flour; mix until smooth, add 1 gill of cream and 1 gill of stock; stir continuously until it boils; take it from the fire, add the beaten yolks of 2 eggs, $\frac{1}{2}$ teaspoon of salt, $\frac{1}{4}$ teaspoon of pepper, and it is ready to serve. Do not boil after adding the yolks.

SAUCE HOLLANDAISE.—*Mrs. W. B. Bradford.*

1 heaping tablespoon butter; when melted, add 1 tablespoon flour, and cook a few minutes. Then add 1 teacup of boiling water, and stir until smooth. Gradually add the yolks of 2 or 3 eggs, the juice of 1 lemon, salt, and red pepper. Nice for fish or meat.

HORSE-RADISH SAUCE.—*Mrs. Geo. Boyd.*

Ingredients: 3 or 4 tablespoons of cream, 4 tablespoons of grated horse-radish, 1 teaspoon of pounded sugar, 1 teaspoon of salt, ½ teaspoon of pepper, 2 teaspoons of mustard, vinegar. Mode: Grate the horse-radish, and mix it well with the sugar, salt, pepper, and the mustard which has been mixed with vinegar; put in the cream, and warm in a double boiler; do not allow to boil, or it will curdle. With cold meat, serve cold. This sauce will last several days.

DRESSING FOR CHOPS.—*Mrs. R. E. Neil.*

2 pickled cucumbers, 1 pickled onion, 1 tablespoon capers; chop all fine and add 1 tablespoon tomato catsup. Melt 1 tablespoon butter: add to it 2 teaspoons flour, 1 cup of stock and the chopped pickles. Simmer 5 minutes, and pour over the chops. This is nicest with breaded chops.

TOMATO SAUCE.—*Mrs. W. B. Bradford.*

1 pint canned tomatoes, 1 tablespoon butter, 1 tablespoon flour, 8 cloves, and a small slice of onion. Cook tomatoes, cloves and onion 10 minutes. Heat butter in a pan, add the flour, stir until brown; add to the tomatoes, and boil 10 minutes longer; season with salt and pepper, and strain through a sieve.

OYSTER DRESSING.—*Mrs. W. F. Jones.*

Remove all the crust from a baker's stale loaf, and crumb up fine; work in 1 cup of butter, a dash of cayenne, and salt to taste. Add 1 quart of fresh oysters and sufficient strained juice to moisten the dressing. Fill the craw of the turkey, and put the remainder inside.

PLAIN DRESSING.—*Mrs. W. F. Jones.*

Make the same as above, omitting the oysters; season with sage; wet with nice rich milk; chop an onion fine, cook in butter and stock or water, and add, if onions are agreeable, but do not brown the onion. A few olives added makes an agreeable variety.

CHESTNUT DRESSING.—*Mrs. L. A. Lancel.*

1 pound chestnuts boiled, 1 pound beef, ½ pound fresh pork, chopped all together. Season with salt and pepper; add ¼ loaf of baker's bread soaked in water and drained, and 2 beaten eggs.

CHESTNUT DRESSING.—*Mrs. McMahon.*

1 quart chestnuts; shell, blanch, and boil them until tender; strain, mash or chop fine; add 1 tablespoon butter, 1 teaspoon salt, and a saltspoon of pepper. Mix, and put into the turkey. Do not mash too fine. I think it better to chop with a hash knife. Or 1 cup of French chestnuts prepared as above may be added to a rich bread and butter dressing.

Attention Ladies————

If you desire to cook a meal, satisfactorily to yourselves and to the palates of those partaking of it, be sure to obtain none but the best goods, and for the . .

CHOICEST AND FRESHEST

Meats, Sausages, Salted Meats, Lard, Etc.

. . Go to

CHRIS. KLEIN

Wholesale and Retail Butcher

The Leading Butchering Establishment of Marin County.

Cor. B and Second Streets.   San Rafael.

Vegetables.

Rules for Cooking Vegetables.

Put all fresh vegetables to cook into boiling water.

Onions and string beans require more time than other vegetables, 1½ hours at least being required to cook them tender.

STUFFED POTATOES.—*Mrs. J. E. Alexander.*

Bake good-sized potatoes; when done, cut off top (the long way), scoop out the inside and mash; season with butter, cream, salt, pepper, and beaten white of egg; refill the potatoes and brown in oven. Must be eaten immediately.

BROILED POTATOES.—*Mrs. E. B. Mahon.*

Slice cold boiled potatoes, dip them lightly into the white of an egg, then broil; when brown, pour over them a little melted butter, pepper, salt, and chopped parsley.

ESCALOPED POTATOES.—*Mrs. A. A. Smith.*

Use a deep baking dish suitable to place on the table; or a granite pan with a napkin wrapped around it will answer. Slice cold boiled potatoes; place 2 slices of salt pork in the bottom of the dish, then a layer of sliced potatoes; over the top of this sprinkle pepper, salt, and a little flour with a few pieces of butter; repeat this till the dish is full; finish the top with flour and butter; fill with milk, and place in the oven; bake 1 hour. This is a nice dish for lunch.

STUFFED GREEN PEPPERS.—*Mrs. L. A. Lancel.*

Cut off the tops of good fresh peppers; take out all the inside; fill with a mixture of sausage meat mixed with bread crumbs, egg, salt, and a little milk if necessary; put them in a saucepan with some nice stock and a good piece of butter; cover tightly and steam 1½ hours.

STUFFED ONIONS.—*Mrs. W. F. C. Hasson.*

Boil until tender 6 medium-sized onions; take out the hearts and chop them up with some cold beef, reserving the outer parts to be stuffed. Put in a frying-pan a tablespoon of lard, add 4 tomatoes, 1 clove of garlic, ½ minced onion, and ½ green pepper roasted on top of the stove; fry these all together, and add the minced meat and onion; cook a few moments, and add 4 tablespoons of olive oil, a little ground allspice, cloves, and oregano, 1 tablespoon sugar, 1 tablespoon vinegar, some salt, and enough claret to moisten thoroughly. Then add a handful of seeded raisins, about 6 chopped olives, and a hard-boiled egg chopped fine; stuff the onions with this hash. Beat 6 eggs until light, yolks and whites separately; mix them together, sprinkle each onion with flour, and dip into the beaten egg; then fry in a frying-pan with plenty of lard. Put in a stewpan a spoonful of lard, and when hot, add 5 or 6 minced tomatoes, 1 chopped onion, a little green pepper, and a clove of garlic, some oregano, salt, and a little soup stock; let it stew a few minutes, put the stuffed onions in the sauce, and simmer ½ hour.

GREEN CORN FRITTERS.—*Mrs. R. E. Neil.*

1 dozen ears corn grated or scraped; yolks of 4 eggs: 3 tablespoons flour. Fry in lard and butter mixed.

CORN FRITTERS.—*Mrs. A. A. Smith.*

½ can of corn, the same quantity of rolled cracker, 2 eggs beaten separately, a pinch of salt, and pepper. Wet the mixture with milk sufficiently to drop from the spoon; fry in a mixture of butter and lard in a frying-pan.

MACARONI, ITALIAN STYLE.—*Mrs. W. F. Jones.*

Cover 1 pound of macaroni with boiling water; salt it and let it cook until tender or about ½ hour. Drain in a colander and pour into the center of the platter. Have prepared a dressing made of 1 can of sliced mushrooms, 1 quart can of tomatoes, salt, a dash of cayenne. 3 tablespoons butter, 1 cup stock, and 1 tablespoon flour rubbed into the butter. Cook mushrooms and tomatoes ½ hour, then add the other ingredients; cook until it is a thick sauce, and pour it over the macaroni. Serve as entree.

TOMATOES STUFFED WITH HAMBURGER STEAK.—*Mrs. H. O. Howitt.*

Take 12 large, firm and ripe tomatoes: remove the tops with a sharp knife, also the centers; fill with the following mixture: Mix well some Hamburger steak with browned bread crumbs, chopped onion, salt and pepper, and especially butter; be sure that the firm texture of the steak is well broken up; then fill the tomatoes with this mixture, with the centers of the tomatoes added; place the tops on them, bind with a light string, and lay in a kettle in which are placed some strips of bacon: steam for ¾ of an hour; then remove the strings carefully and serve. Be sure they are browned before serving.

EGGS AND TOMATOES.—*Dr. C. B. Brown, S. F.*

Mix 1 tablespoon butter and 1 dessert spoon flour; cook together and add ½ pint of thick tomatoes. When this is hot, add 6 eggs beaten light, 1 teaspoon salt, and ½ teaspoon onion juice.

RICE, SPANISH.—*Mrs. L. A. Lancel.*

Put ½ cup of rice into a pan with 1 heaping tablespoon of lard: let boil until all the kernels turn white: then add 1 quart of tomatoes, 1 green pepper, 1 large onion browned in butter, and salt; if not hot enough, add more pepper.

ASPERGES AUX MILANAISE.—*Mrs. W. F. C. Hasson.*

Boil large, choice asparagus till tender; put a layer of it upon the dish in which it is to be served. Sprinkle with salt, cayenne, and a little grated Parmesan: make three layers of this and pour over all a

VEGETABLES. 51

little melted butter; then break on top a fresh egg for each person, and put in the oven until set. Serve very hot.

CREAMED MUSHROOMS.—*Dr. C. B. Brown, S. F.*

1 pound mushrooms, 2 tablespoons butter. Put mushrooms into melted butter, and cook until soft. Add 1 gill cream, 1 teaspoon salt, and a dash of white pepper.

NOODLES A LA GERMAN.—*Mrs. Thos. Duffy.*

2 eggs beaten light; add 2 tablespoons water. Put some flour in a bowl, add the egg, beating well; add more flour to make stiff; knead light like bread; roll thin as possible; leave it dry; then cut in strips 2 inches wide, lay rows together, cut very fine; shake them out on a cloth to dry. Boil 20 minutes in salt water; drain in colander. Fry small cubes of bread in butter; melt more butter, and pour over noodles. Serve immediately.

CAULIFLOWER, GERMAN STYLE.—*Mrs. H. O. Howitt.*

Boil a large white head of cauliflower in salted water until tender; then place it in a baking dish, and pour over it this mixture: the beaten yolks of 2 eggs mixed with a little cream or milk, 2 heaping tablespoons of grated cheese, a little melted butter, a pinch of cayenne pepper, a pinch of salt; bake 5 minutes until brown; serve in same dish. This may be used as an entree.

SAUCE FOR HOT SLAW.—*Mrs. W. F. Jones.*

1 teacup of cream, butter the size of a walnut. When hot mix with a beaten egg, and pour over cabbage that has been cooked in vinegar and water. Pour the hot cream over the egg to prevent curdling.

THE ——

San Rafael,
Cal.

New England Villa

Hotel and Cottages.

Superior Accommodations for Families
Large and shady Grounds . . . . .
Table first-class.   Terms $1.25 to $1.50 per day. $7.00 to $10.00 per week.   .
Children under 12 years, half-price   .

ONE BLOCK FROM
NARROW GAUGE DEPOT.

M. O'CONNOR,
Prop.

GERMEA

For Breakfast.

Cooks in
Three Minutes.

PREPARED FROM THE CHOICEST

CALIFORNIA WHITE WHEAT.

Salads.

CHICKEN SALAD.—*Mrs. F. M. Angellotti.*

2 boiled chickens cut in dice: with this mix thoroughly an equal quantity of good crisp celery cut in small pieces, 3 chopped olives, and 2 teaspoons of capers. Make a dressing of 6 tablespoons of best olive oil, 2 tablespoons of vinegar, 2 teaspoons of salt, and a dash of cayenne; pour over and set away. Prepare a mayonnaise as follows: 2 yolks of eggs in a soup plate; add little by little the olive oil, stirring steadily with a silver fork; as the dressing thickens, thin it with a little lemon juice to the consistency of cream; add salt and pepper to taste. Make a mound, pour over it the mayonnaise, and garnish with lettuce leaves.

CHICKEN SALAD.—*Mrs. J. E. Alexander.*

Cut the white meat of the chicken into small bits (also the dark meat if you wish), cut the celery the same size, and use the same quantity of each; allow 2 hard boiled eggs to each quart of meat. Dressing: 1 teaspoon sugar, 1 teaspoon salt, 2 teaspoons mustard; hot water to mix smooth: ½ cup melted butter, 3 eggs well beaten, ⅔ cup cream, ½ cup vinegar. After it is thoroughly cool add ½ pint olive oil, 1 drop at a time. The dressing must not be put on until just before serving.

SUMMER SALAD.—*Mrs. J. E. Alexander.*

Lay a few crisp lettuce leaves on each plate, then add a few slices ripe tomato and cucumber, cover with salad dressing and serve very cold.

MOSAIC SALAD.—*Mrs. W. F. Jones.*

Prepare and boil separately in salt water, asparagus, cauliflower, string beans, carrots, potatoes, and beets. Cut off the asparagus tips, break up the cauliflower, cut the string beans in small pieces, and cut carrots, potatoes, and beets in any shape fancied. To these ingredients add a few stoned olives, capers, and tiny pickles; baste with French dressing, and set away for an hour in a cold place. To 1 quart of these vegetables take ½ box of Knox's gelatine and soak in a little cold water; then pour over it 1 pint of boiling water, when cool stir into it 1 cup of mayonnaise; pour this over the vegetables, and turn into a mold previously wet in cold water. When set, turn on a platter, garnish with nice white lettuce leaves, and serve with mayonnaise.

ORANGE SALAD.—*Mrs. McMahon.*

Slice oranges lengthwise, and fill lettuce cups same as for strawberries. Pour over the following dressing: ½ cup vinegar, 2 tablespoons salad oil, 1 teaspoon sugar, a pinch of salt.

SALADS.

FRENCH SALAD.—*Mrs. V. Neale.*

Wash the lettuce well and leave in cold water a couple of hours; then dry in a cloth. Mix in the salad bowl 2 tablespoons of olive oil, 4 or 5 drops of vinegar, ½ a small green onion cut in slices, ½ a mild green pepper (when in season), a pinch of salt, and plenty of fresh ground pepper; then break up the best part of 2 lettuce heads into the bowl; mix all well together, and serve. Do not keep it waiting long, and be very careful not to use too much vinegar or salt.

CABBAGE SALAD.—*Miss Parsons, Tamalpais.*

1 cup vinegar, 3 teaspoons mustard (small), 3 eggs, 1 tablespoon melted butter, 1 teaspoon salt, ½ teaspoon pepper, ½ cup sugar. Heat the vinegar in a double boiler, and stir in the other ingredients which have been mixed together. Cook only long enough to thicken slightly, as it curdles if cooked too long. Use this as a dressing to pour over chopped cabbage.

PINK SALAD.—*Mrs. A. A. Smith.*

3 quarts of cabbage chopped very fine, 1 quart of boiled beets chopped, 1 cup of grated horse-radish, 1 teaspoon of black pepper. 1 cup of sugar, 1 tablespoon of salt, ¼ teaspoon red pepper: cover with cold vinegar, and keep in air-tight fruit jars.

GELATINE SALAD.—*Mrs. Oge.*

Soak ½ box Cox's gelatine in 1 cup cold water 1 hour. Boil soup vegetables with 3 whole cloves, season with pepper and salt; put them into 1 quart strained tomatoes; strain the boiling mixture and stir the gelatine into it while heating slowly on the stove; strain again and fill sherbet glasses ½ full. When cold, turn out on salad plates and garnish with lettuce. Serve with mayonnaise dressing.

DEVILED EGGS.—*Mrs. W. F. Jones.*

Boil 8 eggs hard, and lay in cold water until cold. Take off the shells, cut in halves, slicing off a small piece of the big end to make them stand. Remove the yolks and rub smooth; add a little mustard, a tablespoon of butter, a dash of cayenne, and a few drops of vinegar or lemon juice, also salt; make any additions that may be liked. Fill the whites with this mixture and put together; stand them in a bed of chopped cress, lettuce or white cabbage, seasoned with salt, pepper, vinegar, and sugar if desirable. A little chopped ham is nice added. Mayonnaise alone is nice mixed with the yolks, then piled up in the little white cups of the eggs and served on lettuce leaves: in this way cut off both ends of the eggs, so the cups will stand.

STRAWBERRY SALAD.—*Mrs. McMahon.*

Choose the heart leaves of nice head lettuce; make cups of 2 leaves with the stems crossed; fill with firm berries. Put a spoonful of mayonnaise dressing on top of berries.

CELERY SALAD.—*Mrs. Oge.*

Take the white parts of a bunch of celery and cut them into pieces of a quarter of an inch; also cut up a little of the white part of a head of lettuce, and a very little of the top of an onion. Make a mayonnaise

SALADS.

dressing of ¼ cup of olive oil, yolks of 2 eggs, red and black pepper to taste: and when done add 3 tablespoons of thick sweet cream or whipped cream. Mix with the salad and fill small green peppers with the mixture; put one pepper on each plate, and garnish with small pieces of lettuce.

CELERY SALAD.—*Mrs. W. F. Jones.*

Peel 1 dozen nice large tomatoes: remove the seeds and juice, leaving them cup shaped. Cut the nice white stalks from 3 heads of celery into small pieces; baste with French dressing, and set away for an hour in a cold place. Stuff the tomatoes with the celery, sprinkle with salt, and on the top put mayonnaise. Serve very cold on nice crisp lettuce. Celery is also nice served on lettuce leaves with mayonnaise, without tomatoes.

SALAD DRESSING WITHOUT OIL.

1 tablespoon vinegar, the yolk of 1 egg beaten. Put on vinegar to boil, add yolk of egg and stir until it thickens; then add ½ teaspoon mustard, ¼ teaspoon salt, 1 teaspoon sugar, a piece of butter the size of a walnut. Pour all this over the beaten white of the egg, and then add cream until thin enough.

SALAD DRESSING TO KEEP ON HAND.—*Mrs. A. A. Smith.*

5 teaspoons of mustard, 4 teaspoons of sugar, 1 small teaspoon of salt. 4 tablespoons of olive oil: beat these thoroughly; then add 4 eggs, 12 tablespoons of milk, 12 tablespoons of vinegar: stir all together in a quart bowl that can be placed over a boiling kettle; stir constantly till it becomes creamy: remove, and stir a little more lest the eggs curdle. This will keep two months or longer, in an air-tight fruit jar.

CREAM DRESSING FOR SHRIMPS.—*Mrs. W. F. Jones.*

Whip 1 teacup of cream just turning sour; add very little vinegar, and sugar to give a rich taste but not too sweet; pour over the shrimps and serve on lettuce leaves. Nice where one does not like oil; also nice with plain salad.

CREAM DRESSING.—*Mrs. E. B. Mahon.*

1 cup of cream, 1 tablespoon of vinegar, 1 teaspoon of mustard, a little salt: mix together very slowly.

DEVILED EGGS.—*Mrs. E. B. Mahon.*

Boil the eggs 15 minutes, put in cold water to cool, remove the shells, cut them in two lengthwise, take out the yolks and rub to a smooth paste with 1 teaspoon of mustard and 1 teaspoon of salad oil; mix a tablespoon of minced ham with salt and pepper to taste, fill the whites with this mixture (depends on how many eggs in regard to mixture).

WALNUT SANDWICHES.—*Mrs. J. M. Dollar.*

Mix finely chopped walnuts with enough mayonnaise dressing to make a soft paste. Take thin slices of buttered bread, spread 1 slice with the paste, put a lettuce leaf on the other; put them together, and cut in any shapes desired. Keep in a cold place until ready to use them.

DR. G. G. VANDERLIP

Dentist

OFFICE HOURS:

    9 to 12 A. M.,
    1 to 4.30 P. M.

OFFICE:

    Over Inman's Drug Store,

SAN RAFAEL.

HEPBURN WILKINS

Attorney at Law

619 FOURTH STREET,
Wilkins' Building.

San Rafael,
Marin Co., Cal.

C. ROY BARNEY

San Rafael,
Cal.

Insurance and General Commission Agent

813 FOURTH ST.

BET. C AND D.

Cheese.

SARDINES WITH CHEESE.—*Mrs. Carter. P. Pomeroy.*

Open a box of large sardines, drain them; cut stale bread into ½-inch slices, then into strips a little longer than the sardines; fry in deep fat a bright brown, drain on brown paper. On each strip lay one sardine, and cover with grated Parmesan cheese. Put in hot oven on pan till the cheese melts and crusts over them; sprinkle with finely chopped parsley and a little lemon juice: serve hot.

EGGS BAKED IN CHEESE SAUCE.—*Mrs. Carter P. Pomeroy.*

1 teaspoon of butter melted; add 1 teaspoon of flour, or more if a thicker sauce is liked. Cook thoroughly but do not brown; add 1 cup of milk, or cream preferred (use more butter if milk is used), which must be added slowly to make a smooth sauce; then add 4 tablespoons of grated cheese; stir well, and when thoroughly hot, pour into a hot baking dish which can go to the table. Drop in 4 eggs as if for poaching, being very careful not to break the yolks. Put at once into oven, and when the eggs are set serve at once. Makes a very nice entree.

CHEESE SOUFFLE.—*Mrs. W. F. Jones.*

2 tablespoons of butter, 1 tablespoon of flour. Rub smooth, and add ½ cup of milk, yolks of 3 eggs, and 1 cup of grated cheese. Cook in double boiler; let boil 2 minutes, and then cool. Add the beaten whites, and bake 10 minutes in muffin rings with white paper underneath. Remove rings and serve immediately on the paper. Delicious.

CHEESE SCALLOP.—*Mrs. Robert Dollar.*

Soak 1 cup of dry bread crumbs in fresh milk. Beat into this 3 eggs; add 1 tablespoon of butter and ½ pound of grated cheese; strew sifted bread crumbs upon the top, and bake in the oven a delicate brown.

MACARONI.—*Mrs. R. E. Neil.*

Boil macaroni until tender, and drain through a colander; then turn it into a pudding dish and pour over it 1 cup of rich gravy, 1 cup of stewed tomatoes, 1 cup of dried mushrooms that have been soaked in warm water 2 hours, and 1 teaspoon of salt in which has been rubbed a little garlic. Lastly, add 2 chopped Chili peppers and 2 cups of grated Parmesan cheese spread over the top. Bake ½ or ¾ of an hour. Excellent.

MACARONI CROQUETTES.—*Mrs. Carter P. Pomeroy.*

2 ounces macaroni, butter size ½ an egg, pepper and salt, 1 tablespoon cream, 2 ounces grated cheese. Boil macaroni in water ¾ of an hour;

strain, and cut in small pieces; put back in stewpan with the cream and butter; when hot, add cheese and 1 egg well beaten. Put away till cold; shape into croquettes, roll in egg and bread crumbs, and fry in deep lard. This is very good: use small macaroni; serve alone, or with a tomato or cheese sauce.

MACARONI AND CHEESE.—*Mrs. W. F. Jones.*

Boil ¾ of a pound of macaroni in salt and water for about ½ hour or until tender, and drain through a colander. Grate ¾ of a pound of rich cheese. Put a layer of macaroni in the bottom of an earthenware dish; add salt, a few pieces of butter, a dash of cayenne, and sprinkle with cheese. Repeat until your material is all used, having cheese come on top. Pour over this 1 pint of milk and bake about ½ hour. It must be well browned and the milk cooked away, but not too dry. Serve as an entree.

CHEESE STRAWS.—*Mrs. W. F. C. Hasson.*

Mix together 2 ounces grated Parmesan cheese, 2 ounces flour, 2 ounces butter, and a little salt and cayenne: make into a stiff paste with the yolk of 1 egg. Roll out the paste until ⅛ inch thick and 5 inches wide; cut into strips ⅛ inch wide, and bake on buttered tin in a hot oven 10 minutes or till a pale brown.

CHEESE STRAWS.—*Mrs. W. F. Jones.*

1 cup of flour, ½ scant cup of butter, 1 cup of rich grated cheese, a pinch of salt. Rub flour and butter together as for pastry, then add cheese, 5 dashes of cayenne: wet with the whites of 2 eggs well beaten, and if not moist enough to roll, add a little water. The eggs can be omitted and all water used. Roll out as for rather thick pie-crust, and cut in strips 2 inches wide; then cut these into strips ¼ of an inch wide. Bake in a quick oven until a light brown. They must be crisp. Nice with salad or cold meats. Keep in tightly closed tins.

WELSH RAREBIT.—*Mrs. W. F. Jones.*

Melt 1 cup of grated cheese in a saucepan; add 2 beaten eggs, 2 tablespoons cream, and lastly a dash of cayenne and of mustard. Stir constantly until done, and serve immediately on hot buttered toast; it is best served on hot individual plates. For a Golden Buck place a poached egg on top of each serving. A little ale may be added at the last moment to the plain Rarebit, and served bubbling hot.

ADVERTISEMENTS. 61

Burtchaell & Co.

... The ...

Leading Grocers

⚜

Crockery, Glassware,
Agate and Tinware.   622, 624 Fourth St.

San Rafael, California.

C. Grosjean & Co.

•———— GROCERS ————•

KEEP THE BEST

Baking Powder, Extracts,

Gelatines,

Corn Starch, Etc., Etc.

To be be used in the following recipes.

Telephone Red 34.   715, 717, Fourth St.

Eggs.

OMELETTE.—*Mrs. Wm. B. Bradford.*

Beat the whites and yolks of 6 eggs separately. To the yolks add 3 teaspoons of corn starch or flour, salt, and 1 cup of milk. Stir in the whites and turn into a hot buttered pan. When it sets put it on the top slide of the oven for a few minutes, then fold and serve. A little chopped parsley or finely chopped ham makes a variety, or a few cooked green peas, or a few fresh oysters seasoned and cooked in their own juice until the gills curl, and spread over the omelette just before serving. Nice for an entree.

OMELETTE.—*Mrs. Carter P. Pomeroy.*

Sure to be good and light. 6 eggs, yolks and whites beaten separately; ½ tablespoon of butter; ½ tablespoon of flour; 1 cup of milk; make a white sauce of milk, butter and flour, and when cold add first the yolks well beaten and then the whites beaten to a stiff froth; have the pan very hot, brown quickly, fold and serve. If possible put the pan in oven for a moment as it cooks more quickly. This makes a delicious entree with a little canned or green corn left from the day before, made hot and folded inside; or a little stewed tomato; or some asparagus tips cooked in a cream sauce: or as a dessert with lumps of sugar on the edge of the dish, upon which brandy or rum has been poured and lighted; bring it burning to the table, and with the serving spoon throw the burning brandy over the omelette.

CHOCOLATE OMELETTE.—*Mrs. W. F. Jones.*

Make either of the above omelettes, and just before folding, pour over the following; 2 heaping tablespoons chocolate, 1 tablespoon sugar, and 1 of water; cook until smooth. Serve as dessert.

SPANISH OMELETTE.—*Mrs. Walter S. Hobart.*

Put 2 large tablespoons butter with 2 large bell-peppers chopped fine, into a frying-pan with 6 or 7 large tomatoes skinned and chopped. Cook till tender; add 2 or 3 large onions; cook all together until tender; season with salt, and red or black pepper to suit taste. Make an omelette of 1 or 2 eggs to each person; when partly done add the above filling, and make a turnover.

SWEETBREAD OMELETTE.—*Mrs. L. A. Lancel.*

Boil and skin a pair of sweetbreads, and cut in small pieces; brown some butter; put in the sweetbreads, when brown pour over it the eggs prepared as for any omelette; add a little chopped green onion and parsley.

SALADS.

EGGS WITH MUSTARD SAUCE.—*Mrs. Wm. Lichtenberg.*

Boil as many eggs as needed, 5 minutes; take off the shells and cut in halves lengthwise; lay on a platter. Melt a slice of butter; mix a little mustard with milk, and add to the heated butter; as this will curdle, boiling water must be added to make it smooth. Pour this gravy over the eggs, and serve hot for lunch.

BAKED EGGS.—*Mrs. W. F. Jones.*

Chop very fine some cold meat; lamb or veal is preferable. Put in a saucepan with a good piece of butter, salt and pepper, and add enough gravy stock or milk to moisten. When hot, have muffin rings in a pan, and drop into each one enough of the mixture to about half fill the ring; then drop a fresh egg on the top of each, not breaking the yolks: put some pieces of butter with salt and pepper over the top, and bake until the eggs are cooked. Slip out of the rings and serve. This can be made in a large dish without muffin rings.

CREAMED EGGS.—*Mrs. J. L. Tharp.*

3 eggs for 5 guests; boil 10 minutes, then lay in cold water to cool. Prepare toast cut in any fancy shapes desired. Put 1 pint of cream to heat, not boil. Separate whites from yolks of eggs; press whites through fruit presser, then add to cream. Have toast arranged upon a platter; having pressed yolks through fruit presser, pile upon each piece of toast; pour cream around; add salt and pepper to taste. Serve immediately.

EGGS ON ANCHOVY TOAST.—*Mrs. Carter P. Pomeroy*

Cut round pieces of toast, butter them and spread with anchovy paste. Make a cupful of good rich cream sauce; chop the whites of 5 hard boiled eggs fine; put them into the cream sauce, heap it on the toast; squeeze the yolks of the eggs through a patent potato masher of the squeezing kind, and pile that on top. Serve hot on individual plates as an entree, or arrange with a garnish of parsley on a large platter; it is pretty and good, and easily made.

EGGS WITH ANCHOVY CREAM SAUCE.—*Mrs. Carter P. Pomeroy.*

Make a large cupful of cream sauce; add enough anchovy sauce to color it pink, about the color of shrimps, and either poach eggs in it, or put the sauce in a hot baking dish, drop the eggs carefully in, set in hot oven, and when the eggs have set, serve on same dish: or boil the eggs hard, cut in halves, arrange neatly on a dish, and pour the sauce around them: making 3 quite distinct dishes, and all good.

ANCHOVIED EGGS.—*Dr. C. B. Brown, S. F.*

2 tablespoons butter and 1 tablespoon flour; stir until smooth; ½ pint of milk and 2 teaspoons anchovy paste. Stir until smooth and thick, then add 6 hard boiled eggs cut in slices, 1 tablespoon cream, and a dash of cayenne. Cook in double boiler.

SMOTHERED EGGS.—*Mrs. W. F. Jones.*

Have a large spoonful of butter hot, and the pan hot; set this on back of stove, break in the eggs quickly, and cover; keep turning the pan so that all will get the same heat. Peep in once in a while, and when you see the white set, remove cover and dish up carefully. Delicious if done properly.

THE MOST DELICATE AND WHOLESOME WAY TO BOIL EGGS.—*Mrs. W. F. Jones.*

Put them in a saucepan, pour fast boiling water over them, cover tightly, and remove at once to back of stove: let stand 8 minutes, or 10 if required harder.

Puddings.

PLUM PUDDING.—*Mrs. Vincent Neale.*

Ingredients: 1 pound seeded raisins, ½ pound sultanas, 1 pound currants, 1¼ pounds moist sugar (brown), 1½ pounds bread crumbs, 12 eggs, 1½ pounds finely chopped suet, ½ pound mixed candied peel, rind of 1 lemon, a pinch of nutmeg and cinnamon, a few drops of almond flavor, 1 wineglass of whiskey or brandy. Cut the raisins, but do not chop them; cut the candied peel in thin slices; wash and pick the currants, and dry them; mix all the ingredients together and moisten with the eggs (if too moist, sprinkle a little flour over); stir in the brandy. Scald and flour a pudding cloth, put in the pudding and tie up fairly tight; boil for 6 hours. 2 or 3 puddings may be made instead of 1, as they will keep for several weeks if hung up in a dry, cool place. Excellent.

PLUM PUDDING.—*Mrs. J. E. Alexander.*

1 pound butter, 1 pound suet chopped fine and free from shreds, 1 pound sugar, 2½ pounds flour, 2 pounds raisins seeded and chopped fine and dredged with flour, 2 pounds currants carefully washed, ¼ pound citron finely shredded, 12 eggs, whites and yolks beaten separately, 1 pint milk, 1 cup brandy, ½ ounce cloves, ½ ounce mace, 2 grated nutmegs. Beat together cream, butter and sugar, and mix in the yolks when beaten smooth and light. Add the milk, then the flour alternately with the beaten whites. Then add the brandy and spice, and lastly the fruit well dredged with flour. Mix all thoroughly. Wring out pudding cloth in hot water, flour well inside, pour in the mixture, and boil 5 hours.

ENGLISH PLUM PUDDING.—*A. E. Menzies.*

1 pound raisins, 1 pound currants, 1 pound beef suet chopped very fine, ½ pound brown sugar, ½ pound flour, ¾ pound bread crumbs (stale bread), ¼ pound mixed peel (orange, lemon, and citron), 1 teaspoon salt, 1 teaspoon mixed spices, and 8 eggs. Mix all the ingredients very thoroughly. Wring a cloth out of boiling water, and flour it. After putting the pudding into the cloth, tie tightly, but allow room to swell. Boil 10 or 12 hours.

PLUM PUDDING.—*Mrs. Robert Dollar.*

2 pounds raisins, 1 pound currants, 1 pound beef suet, 2 ounces orange peel, 2 ounces lemon peel, 2 ounces sweet almonds, 2 ounces bitter almonds, 1 pound bread crumbs, the rind and juice of one lemon, ¾ pound flour, 1 pound sugar, 1 tumbler of jelly, 9 eggs, ½ teaspoon soda. Boil 9 hours. This quantity may be made into several puddings, and cooked a shorter time.

PUDDINGS.

ENGLISH PLUM PUDDING.—*Mrs. French.*

1 pound suet shredded and minced, 1½ pounds raisins stoned and cut, 1½ pounds currants washed, 1 pound stale bread crumbs grated, 1 pound sugar, ½ pint brandy, 12 eggs beaten light; ¼ pound of citron, orange and lemon peel, 1 nutmeg grated, 1 spoon ginger, cloves, and cinnamon. Mix ½ hour with the hand. Flour and butter a cloth which is just dipped in hot water: put the pudding in and tie tightly; boil 5 to 8 hours; blanch some almonds, put them endwise 2 inches apart over the top; after it is on the dish, pour some brandy over: and just as it is to be brought to the table, set fire to the brandy that the pudding may be in flames.

ANY-DAY PLUM PUDDING.—*Miss A. Gordon.*

1 cup of sweet milk, 1 cup of molasses, 1 cup each of raisins and currants, 1 cup of suet chopped fine (or, instead, a small cup of butter), 1 teaspoon of salt and 1 teaspoon of soda sifted with 3 cups of flour, 1 teaspoon each of cinnamon and allspice. Mix milk, molasses, suet, and spice; add flour, and then the fruit. Put in a buttered mold, and boil 3 hours. Serve with hard or liquid sauce.

FIG PUDDING.—*Mrs. Wm. Lichtenberg.*

¾ pound of grated bread, ¾ pound of best figs, 6 ounces of suet chopped, 6 ounces of moist sugar, 1 egg, a little nutmeg, 1 teacup of milk. The figs and suet must be chopped very fine: mix the bread and suet first, then add the figs, sugar, and nutmeg, after that the egg and the milk. Put into a basin and boil 4 hours. Serve with brandy sauce.

FIG PUDDING.—*Mrs. Carter P. Pomeroy.*

¾ cup of finely chopped suet, 2 cups of stale bread crumbs, 2 eggs well beaten, 1 teaspoon each of cloves, cinnamon, and ginger, a little salt, 1 cup of sugar, ½ pound of chopped dried figs. Steam 3 hours. It is best served with the wine sauce given with the Cottage pudding.

TROY PUDDING.—*A. E. Menzies.*

1 cup of suet, 1 cup of flour, 1 cup of milk, 1 cup of currants, ½ cup of molasses, 1 teaspoon of baking powder, and a small pinch of salt. Boil for 3 hours.

STEAMED NUT PUDDING.—*Mrs. W. F. Jones.*

Mix thoroughly together 1 cup chopped walnuts, 1 cup chopped raisins, 1 cup currants, 1 cup New Orleans molasses, ½ cup brown sugar, 3 eggs, 1 cup chopped suet, 1½ cups sour milk; sift 1 teaspoon soda and 1 teaspoon yeast powder with 2 cups flour, ½ teaspoon each of cinnamon, allspice and cloves. Pour into a buttered mold that will be about half full to allow for rising. Steam 3 hours.

SPICE PUDDING.—*Mrs. A. A. Smith.*

Put ½ cup of butter and lard mixed, into a mixing bowl; add to this 1 cup of sugar, 1 well beaten egg, 1 teaspoon ground cinnamon, ¼ grated nutmeg, 1 teaspoon each of allspice and cloves; beat all well together. Pour into this ½ cup of molasses, 1 cup of cold coffee, and 1 cup of flour with 3 teaspoons of baking powder sifted thoroughly; add enough flour to make a stiff batter; put into this mixture 1 cup of stoned raisins and 1½ cups of currants; add flour enough to barely mold with the hands, then turn into a floured cloth and pin loosely, giving room to swell. Place in boiling water and boil 1 hour.

SUET PUDDING.—*Mrs. R. E. Neil.*

1 cup of suet chopped fine, 1 cup of molasses, 1 cup of sour milk, 3 cups of flour, 1 teaspoon soda dissolved in the milk: spice highly, and steam 3 hours.

FREE CHURCH PUDDING.—*Mrs. A. E. Menzies.*

1 breakfast cup of beef suet; the same of flour, bread crumbs, raisins or currants; 1 teacup of brown sugar; 1 teacup of milk; 1 teaspoon of soda; ¼ a nutmeg grated. Boil 3 hours.

STEAMED FRUIT PUDDING.—*Mrs. W. F. Jones.*

1 cup of sweet milk, 2 tablespoons butter rubbed with 1 cup of sugar, 2 eggs, 3 cups of flour sifted with 3 teaspoons baking powder. Mix, and then add 1 cup of preserved figs, or dried figs chopped and stewed until tender, or any other fruit you may prefer, making some allowance about the fruit being dry or juicy, as to the stiffness of the batter. Fill teacups about half full, and steam ½ hour. Turn each mold upon a plate, and serve hot with cream; or sauce can be used if preferable.

COTTAGE PUDDING.—*Mrs. Carter P. Pomeroy.*

Put in mixing bowl first 3 tablespoons melted butter, 1 cup sugar, 1 beaten egg, 1 light pint of flour with 2 teaspoons baking powder sifted with it, and 1 cup of sweet milk last of all. This will seem thin, but will make a nice loaf, light and tender. Serve hot with wine or other sauce.

BOILED COTTAGE PUDDING.—*Mrs. W. B. Bradford.*

1 cup of sugar, 1 tablespoon butter, 2 eggs, 1 cup of milk, 3 cups of flour, or enough to make a stiff batter, 1 teaspoon salt, 2 teaspoons yeast powder. Boil in buttered mold 1 hour. Serve with hard sauce.

GOLDEN PUDDING.

1 teacup each of finely chopped suet, and of sugar; 1 breakfast cup bread crumbs; 2 tablespoons orange marmalade; 3 eggs. Boil 2 hours. To be eaten with hard sauce.

OLD-FASHIONED RICE PUDDING.—*Mrs. Thos. Duffy.*

2 tablespoons rice to 1 quart of milk; 2 tablespoons sugar, a grating of nutmeg, ¼ cup of raisins if liked; cook slowly for 1½ hours in a moderate oven, stirring down crust for the first hour as fast as it forms. Then allow a paper-like cover to form, and the pudding is done. Serve cold. Can be made on Saturday for Sunday dinner.

RICE PUDDING.

½ cup of rice boiled in 1 cup of water with a little salt; cover tightly and cook slowly 20 minutes; then add 1 pint of milk, let it come to a boil, and add the yolks of 3 well beaten eggs, also ⅔ cup of seedless raisins chopped, and 5 tablespoons of sugar. Put in buttered pan; set in the oven until the custard sets, then cover with the well beaten whites with 2 tablespoons of sugar and a little vanilla; brown in oven.

BREAD PUDDING.—*Mrs. A. E. Menzies.*

1 quart of milk, 2 tumblers of bread crumbs, 4 eggs, 2 cups of sugar, 2 lemons, 1 slice of butter. Beat the yolks separately, and mix with milk and bread crumbs; add 1 cup of sugar, the rind of the lemons, and butter. Boil until thick as a custard. Boil 1 cup of sugar and juice of lemons separately. Beat whites of the eggs, add juice, and spread on the top for a meringue. Brown in the oven.

CORN MEAL PUDDING.—*Mrs. Daniel Bradford.*

1 pint of milk; as it comes to a boil, stir in ½ cup of meal. When cold, add 3 well beaten eggs, ⅔ of a cup of molasses, ½ teaspoon of salt, 1 wineglass of wine, butter size of half an egg, ½ teaspoon of soda. Beat well, and add less than 1 quart of cold milk. Bake 3 hours with a cover over it, and stir it every half hour until the last hour. Very nice.

BATTER PUDDING.—*Mrs. McMahon.*

1 quart of milk, 10 tablespoons flour, 7 eggs, 1 teaspoon salt, ½ teaspoon soda, 1 teaspoon cream tartar; bake 40 minutes; eat with hard sauce.

LEMON TOAST.—*Mrs. W. F. Jones.*

Beat the yolks of 3 eggs and add 1½ cups of sweet milk. Dip thin slices of bread in this, and fry a light brown in butter.

SAUCE.—Beat the whites of 3 eggs stiff; add ½ cup of white sugar, the juice of 1 lemon and 1 cup of boiling water. Pour over the toast as you serve it.

QUEEN ESTHER'S TOAST.—*Mrs. A. E. Menzies.*

Cut stale bread into pieces 2 inches square and 1 inch thick. Steep them well in milk, then dip in beaten yolk of egg, and fry in butter. Make a sauce of sugar, water and cinnamon, to serve with the toast.

BERRY PUDDING.—*Mrs. E. B. Mahon.*

2 eggs, 1 pint of milk, a little salt, ½ cup of sugar, flour to make a thick batter, 1 teaspoon yeast powder, 1 pint of berries (any kind) well dredged with flour, stirred in at the last; boil 1 hour in mold. Make sauce.

BLACKBERRY OR RASPBERRY PUDDING.—*Mrs. W. F. Jones.*

Put a layer of berries in the bottom of a baking dish and sprinkle with sugar; then cover with a layer of thin bread and butter, and repeat until the dish is full; have the last layer of bread crumbs. If made from canned fruit, drain off the juice and pour it over the pudding last, then the sugar may not be needed. Bake in a pan of water in rather a slow oven about 1 hour. The blackberry pudding is best hot with hard sauce. The raspberry pudding is to be eaten cold with cream.

STRAWBERRY SHORTCAKE.—*Mrs. W. F. Jones.*

Sieve well together 1 quart of flour, 1 level teaspoon salt, and 2 heaping teaspoons baking powder; rub in ½ cup of butter; then wet up with milk just sufficient to roll out. Divide the dough into 4 parts; roll 1 piece in a round shape, put in a deep jelly cake pan, spread the top with a little butter; roll out another piece and pile on top of this; prepare the other 2 pieces the same way in another pan, and bake in rather a quick oven until nice and brown. Then remove from the oven; open and spread both sides generously with butter. Have a drawer of berries cut up and well sugared; put half between each shortcake and serve at once with rich cream. It is an improvement to halve enough of the largest berries to put around the edge of the shortcake, pouring berries inside; then cover the top with whipped cream.

PEACH COBBLER.—*Mrs. E. B. Mahon.*

Fill a pie dish with peeled peaches leaving in the pits; add a very little cold water and sugar to taste. Cover with pie crust, prick with a fork; bake ¾ of an hour. Eat with cream.

PEACH PUDDING.—*Mrs. W. F. Jones.*

Peel and halve 1 dozen peaches, and sweeten to taste; or use 1 quart of canned peaches; place in a pudding dish and put in the oven. Cream the yolks of 4 eggs and 1 cup of sugar; add 1 tablespoon water, 1 teaspoon lemon extract, and 1½ cups of flour into which 1 teaspoon of baking powder has been sifted, and the whites of the eggs beaten stiff. Pour over the hot peaches and bake about 20 to 30 minutes. Serve hot with cream.

APPLE PUDDING.—*Miss A. Gordon.*

Fill a buttered baking dish with sliced apples, and pour over the top a batter made of 1 tablespoon of butter, ½ cup sugar, 1 egg, ½ cup sweet milk, and 1 cup of flour in which has been sifted 1 teaspoon of baking powder. Bake in a moderate oven till brown. Serve with cream and sugar, or liquid sauce. Blackberries are very nice served in the same way.

STEWED APPLE PUDDING.—*Miss Margaret Bremner.*

Pare and slice as thin as you would for pies 6 medium-sized tart apples (Northern Spies are the best), and lay them in the bottom of a round baking dish. Stir 1 cup of sugar and ¼ cup of butter to a cream; add 2 eggs well beaten, and 1 cup of milk. Sift together 2 cups of flour and 2 teaspoons of baking powder; add the flour to the mixture, and stir well. Cover the apples with the mixture and steam 1 hour; serve with a cream or foaming sauce.

APPLE DUMPLINGS.—*Mrs. W. F. Jones.*

1 pint of flour, 1½ teaspoons baking powder, salt, butter the size of an egg, milk to roll. Cover each apple, or whatever fruit being used, with some of the crust, and put in the oven. Have the dumplings half covered with cold water in which you have put a little butter. Cover the basin and let them steam about 35 minutes; then remove the cover and let them brown 10 minutes, and serve with sauce. This can be rolled out in 1 piece and spread with fruit and made into a roll.

BLACK BREAD PUDDING.

Take yolks of 3 eggs and beat with 1 cup of granulated sugar; add 1 cup of grated stale black bread gradually. Add 1 teaspoon of cinnamon, a pinch of allspice, or a very little ground cloves if desired. Mix all together and then add the beaten whites of the eggs. Bake in a tube form or pudding dish; when baked, leave it in the oven, and pour 1 cup of red wine over it. Serve the pudding with either a Charlotte russe, or a rich wine sauce.

APPLE AND TAPIOCA PUDDING.—*Mrs. E. B. Mahon.*

1 teacup of tapioca soaked well in water over night (about a pint); cook until clear—about ½ hour; add 1 cup of sugar, a little salt, and lemon or nutmeg; when cooked, pour over the apples after paring and quartering them, add a few small pieces of butter over the top to help brown it. Hard sauce, or cream may be served with it.

PARIS SAUCE FOR SWEET PUDDINGS.—*Mrs. E. B. Mahon.*

Take 1 glass of sherry, 1 large tablespoon of powdered sugar, and the well-beaten yolks of 2 eggs; put these in saucepan on fire and stir until thick; add slowly 3 tablespoons of cream, without letting it boil.

FOAM SAUCE.—*Mrs. W. F. Jones.*

2 eggs, butter the size of an egg, 1 cup sugar. Beat the yolks, butter and sugar together thoroughly, add the whites beaten to a stiff froth, the juice of 1 lemon, and ½ cup of boiling water; serve immediately. Very nice with cottage pudding.

FOAMING SAUCE.—*Miss Margaret Bremner.*

Beat to a cream ½ cup of sugar and 1 tablespoon of butter; add 4 tablespoons of cream and a few drops of vanilla. Beat with an egg beater, setting the bowl in a dish of hot water till the sauce is light and foamy. Serve as soon as finished.

COMMON SAUCE.—*Mrs. W. F. Jones.*

1 tablespoon flour and 1 tablespoon butter rubbed together; pour on boiling water until of the right consistency; add 1 cup of sugar, and just before serving, add ½ cup of wine or 2 tablespoons brandy, or any extract preferred. An egg beaten light and added last is an improvement.

WINE SAUCE.—*Mrs. Carter P. Pomeroy.*

2 cups of sugar, ½ cup of butter, 1 cup of sherry with a little brandy. Stir butter and sugar till it creams, adding, drop by drop, the wine. When mixed, put into the dish in which it is to be served, and set in a basin of hot water. Do not stir or disturb it, and when melted it will foam as if made of beaten eggs. This sauce is to be used with cottage, plum, or any hot pudding, and is delicious.

Light Desserts.

GERMAN PUFFS.—*Mrs. E. W. Newhall.*

1 pint of milk, 10 tablespoons of flour, 1 tablespoon of melted butter, 6 eggs, leaving out the whites of 3. Bake in buttered tins half filled, 20 minutes in hot oven. Turn them into a flat dish, and just before serving pour over them the following sauce: Whites of 3 eggs beaten to a stiff froth, 1 coffee cup of sugar, juice of 2 oranges.

CREAM PUFFS.—*Mrs. Wm. Lichtenberg.*

½ cup of butter, 3 eggs, ½ pint of water, a pinch of salt, flour about ¼ pound. Boil the butter, water and salt; add the flour quickly; boil until the dough loosens from the saucepan; if it does not do this quickly, add more flour; let the mixture cool; add the yolks and the whipped whites of 3 eggs. Drop into boiling lard, the size of an egg; fry till brown, and serve with jelly; or bake in oven, and fill with whipped cream.

CREAM PUFFS.—*Mrs. R. E. Neil.*

1 cup water, ½ cup butter, soda the size of a pea. When boiling stir in 1 cup flour, and cook until the mixture will roll in a ball in the pan. Spread out to cool; when cool add, 1 at a time, 3 eggs. Drop into 12 puffs, and bake 25 minutes in a moderate oven.

CREAM PUFF FILLING WITH WALNUTS.—*Mrs. W. F. Jones.*

When whipped cream is not obtainable, make the following custard: 1 pint of milk in a double boiler, 1 cup of sugar, 2 tablespoons of corn starch wet in a little cold milk and added to th boiling milk, 1 teaspoon butter, 2 eggs beaten, 1 teaspoon vanilla and 1 teacup chopped walnuts.

NEW ZEALAND TRIFLE.—*Miss F. Alice Brown.*

Cut a stale sponge cake into slices about an inch thick; then put in layers raspberry jam, about 12 macaroons, 2 dozen ratafias, 2 ounces sweet almonds, grated rind of 1 lemon, ½ pint wine, 6 tablespoons brandy. Cover with good custard, and then with whipped cream. For the whip—1 pint cream, sugar, the whites of 2 eggs, wine to flavor; whip till thick.

A LADY FINGER TRIFLE.—*Mrs. McMahon.*

6 yolks of eggs beaten with a cup of powdered sugar; have on the stove 3½ good wine glasses of sherry and a little water, into which put 1 teaspoon of sugar and 1 of vanilla; stir in the beaten eggs and sugar, then add 1 large teaspoon of flour made into a paste. Have a deep platter lined with lady fingers and macaroons, sprinkle with wine; when the mixture has slightly cooled, pour over the cakes, beat the whites

LIGHT DESSERTS.

with 6 scant tablespoons of sugar, spread over top, let brown in the oven: to be eaten cold.

TRIFLE.—Mrs. A. A. Adair, Riverside, Cal.

Put a layer of cake crumbed up in the dish you expect to serve it in on the table; if the cake is stale and dry put a little hot water over it to soften just a little. If the cake is fresh the fruit juice will be sufficient to moisten it; put in lots of walnuts chopped not very fine, and a generous sprinkling of cocoanut; add strawberries or raspberries; cover with a nice rich custard; then add another generous sprinkling of cocoanut, and cover the top with whipped cream. This is very nice.

BAKED PRUNE PUDDING.—Dr. C. B. Brown, S. F.

Put ½ pound of prunes and 1 slice of bread through a meat cutter together. Add 1 egg, piece of butter size of an egg, milk to fill pudding dish, and ½ cup of sugar. Bake ¾ of an hour.

PRUNE FLOAT.—Miss Tena Bremner.

1 pint milk, 4 tablespoons corn starch, ½ pound prunes, 1 tablespoon sugar, ¼ teaspoon vanilla, 4 eggs, 3 tablespoons powdered sugar. Wash choice prunes in several waters, and soak over night. In the morning add 1 tablespoon granulated sugar, and stew until tender. Cut a few in halves, remove the stones from all, and chop the rest very fine. Put milk on to heat, beat yolks of 4 eggs light with 1 tablespoon of sugar and syrup from prunes; add to hot milk, also the corn starch moistened with a little cold milk; stir until it thickens; then remove from the fire and stir in the chopped prunes and vanilla. Pour into pudding dish in which it is to be served. Beat whites of eggs to a stiff froth with 3 spoonfuls of sugar, and put on top of the pudding through a pastry tube. Drop half prunes around the top. Put into a quick oven, and brown slightly. May be served cold with whipped cream.

PRUNE WHIP.—Mrs. A. A. Adair, Riverside, Cal.

20 prunes cooked without sugar till very tender and very dry; stone and chop fine; beat the whites of 4 eggs very stiff; add a small cup of sugar and ¼ teaspoon of cream of tartar; mix all thoroughly; bake ½ hour in a pan set in a pan of water. Serve with cream; whipped cream is nicest.

PRUNE SOUFFLE.—Mrs. J. L. Tharp.

1 pound French prunes boiled and chopped fine; add 1 teacup of sugar, then the well-beaten whites of 5 eggs. Bake 20 minutes after adding extract of lemon. When cold turn out of pan, and cover with whipped cream.

APPLE SOUFFLE.—Mrs. E. B. Mahon.

Stew the apples, add a little grated lemon peel, the juice, also sugar to sweeten; line the sides and bottom of the dish about 2 inches thick. Make a boiled custard with 1 pint of milk, 2 eggs, and a little sugar; when cool, pour into the center of the dish; beat the whites, add a little sugar, spread over, and brown a few minutes in oven.

OMELETTE SOUFFLE.—*Mrs. W. F. Jones.*

Beat the whites and yolks of 3 eggs separately. To the whites add 2 tablespoons sugar; mix together, flavor with vanilla; put into a pudding dish, sprinkle with sugar, bake 15 minutes, and serve immediately.

SAGO CREAM.—*Mrs. W. F. Jones.*

Cook ½ cup of sago in 1 quart of milk until clear. Then add 1 cup of sugar and the yolks of 3 eggs. When a little cool, stir in the well beaten whites and flavor. Some use the pearl tapioca, and cook it the same way.

DESSERT.—*Mrs. A. A. Smith.*

Slice the ripe part of a watermelon, and cut it into diamonds, squares, hearts, or disks, the size of a mouthful. Put a layer of watermelon in a glass fruit dish, cover with sugar, then another layer of watermelon, and so on till the dish is full, with sugar over the top; set it in the ice-chest till wanted. To be eaten as fruit with cake. This is a delicious way of serving watermelon.

CARAMEL CUSTARD.—*Mrs. W. F. Jones.*

1 quart of milk, 3 eggs, 2 tablespoons corn starch, 1 cup brown sugar. Melt the sugar, stirring constantly; then add the milk but do not let it boil or it will crack. When near boiling add the corn starch, sugar, and yolks of the eggs. When a little cool, stir in the whites and 1 teaspoon vanilla. Pour into a mold; to be eaten with whipped cream.

FLOATING ISLAND.—*Mrs. C. F. Robinson.*

Put 1 quart milk in double boiler; 1 cup sugar, 1 tablespoon of corn starch wet in a little cold milk, are to be added to the milk when boiling. Remove from the fire, add the beaten yolks of 3 eggs; when cool add 1 teaspoon of vanilla, and pour into a glass dish. Just before serving, beat the whites very stiff and drop over the top. This is nice poured over stale cake soaked in wine, over sliced oranges, or over strawberries or raspberries.

BAKED CUSTARD.—*Mrs. W. F. Jones.*

Beat 4 eggs light; add ½ cup of sugar, 1 pint of milk, and nutmeg to taste. When well mixed, pour into a pudding dish and drop into the center ½ cup of nice table syrup; do not stir again. Put into a pan of water and bake in a moderate oven until it sets. When cold, loosen the edges and turn upon a platter. The syrup forms a sauce. If properly made, this is very nice. The use of maple syrup or caramel syrup makes a nice variety. These proportions without the syrup make delicious cup custards, or a nice boiled custard.

LEMON CUSTARD.—*Mrs. W. F. Jones.*

5 eggs, the yolks beaten with 1 large cup of sugar; add the juice and grated rind of 2 lemons. Cook in double boiler, stirring constantly until it bubbles and thickens. Beat the whites to a stiff froth and

gently stir the mixture into them. Dip into lemonade glasses, and serve when cold. This makes about enough for 11 people, and is very delicious.

STRAWBERRY CREAM OR SNOW.—*Mrs. W. F. Jones.*

Whites of 4 eggs beaten to a stiff froth; 1 pint of strawberries passed through a colander and sweetened to taste. Stir gradually and gently into the eggs. Other berries and apple sauce are nice the same way.

DANISH PUDDING.—*Mrs. W. F. Jones.*

Dissolve 1 cup of sago or the same of pearl tapioca in a quart of water, and cook until clear. Add 1 glass of sour jelly or 1 pint of stewed rhubarb, and when cold serve with whipped cream. With the rhubarb do not use quite so much water; but it must not be too stiff or it will be tough. Sweeten to taste.

BAKED BANANAS.—*Mrs. W. F. Jones.*

Cook 1 level tablespoon butter, 2 heaping tablespoons sugar, and the juice of 1 lemon, in a double boiler until clear. Have 1 dozen bananas peeled and sliced once lengthwise on a buttered dish. Pour ½ of this sauce over the bananas, and bake 15 minutes; then add the remainder of the sauce, and bake until a rich brown, basting occasionally. Nice either hot or cold.

BANANAS AND APPLES.—*Mrs. W. F. Jones.*

Pare and core about 1 dozen apples; fill the centers and all the interstices with bananas cut in little squares and stirred into the above sauce. Bake until a rich brown and well done. Serve with cream.

AMBROSIA.—*Mrs. W. F. Jones.*

Peel and slice as many oranges as needed, and fill a glass dish with thin layers alternately of oranges sprinkled with sugar, sliced pineapple and more sugar, then grated cocoanut and more sugar; repeat until the dish is full. Let it stand a few hours before using. Some prefer bananas instead of pineapple, but both will do no harm.

BLANC MANGE.—*Mrs. W. F. Jones.*

1 quart of milk. 1 cup of sugar. 4 tablespoons corn starch wet up in a little milk. When cooked pour it into the beaten whites of 2 eggs, and mold.

SAUCE FOR BLANC MANGE.—1 tablespoon corn starch wet in cold water; pour boiling water over it until it is clear and of the right consistency. Add 1 tablespoon butter, ¾ cup of sugar, the grated rind and juice of 1 lemon, yolks of 2 eggs; then pour around the molded pudding.

CALEDONIA CREAM FOR BLANC MANGE.—Whites of 3 eggs well beaten, 3 tablespoons pulverized sugar, ½ cup of whipped cream, 3 tablespoons of currant and raspberry jelly. Nice without the cream.

DELICIOUS BLANC MANGE.—*Mrs. Wm B. Noble.*

Put 1 ounce of gelatine in a little warm water and keep it on the stove until dissolved; then sweeten and flavor with vanilla 1 quart of cream, and whip it. Strain the gelatine on the cream. Wet the molds in cold water, fill them and set away to congeal.

ARROWROOT BLANC MANGE.—*Mrs. D. Whittemore.*

1 cup milk, 4 teaspoons arrowroot, 2 teaspoons sugar. Make a smooth paste of arrowroot and water; stir this into the boiling milk; add the sugar, flavor with vanilla: stir all the time until it thickens: turn out, and when cold serve with cream.

JELLIED PLUM SYRUP.—*Miss Margaret Bremner.*

Take the juice of any kind of fruit desired. Put ½ a box gelatine to soak in 1 cup of cold water for 20 minutes; add 1 cup of boiling water, and 2 cups of syrup from a can of plums. If the Plymouth Rock gelatine is used, no other acid will be needed, otherwise the juice of ½ a lemon will improve it. Strain all into a large jelly mold, or cups that have been wet with cold water; put on ice or in a cool place until stiff; turn out and serve with cream and sugar or whipped cream. 2 or 3 large plums cut into pieces and put in the jelly while cooking improves the jelly. The writer discovered this recipe while wondering what to do with a can of syrup left over from canning green gages.

EASTER PUDDING.—*Mrs. W. F. Jones.*

Make 1 quart of wine, orange or lemon jelly: mold in a round basin in the center of which you have three saucers turned upside down. Save 1 dozen egg shells opened at the small end, and put them in cold water. Make 1 quart of corn starch blanc mange: fill 3 of the shells, and stand them in a pan of bran or meal. Bruise a few spinach leaves, squeeze out a few drops of the color, add to a little of the mixture, and fill 3 more shells. Color some with chocolate, some with the yolks of eggs and some pink from a little of Knox's pink gelatine. While you are preparing the eggs, have the skin from 2 oranges or 2 lemons boiling; when tender, remove all of the white inside, and cut in little strips with scissors; then boil in syrup until clear, and spread out to dry. The next day turn out the jelly: around the edge of the nest put the peel for straw. Remove the shells from the eggs and pile in the nest: put whipped cream all around the jelly. This is a very pretty dish, and delights the children.

ICED PINEAPPLE CREAM.—*Mrs. W. J. Wickman.*

Take a small ½ box of gelatine: place on fire with 1 cup or 1½ cups of water, and allow to dissolve. After thoroughly dissolved, strain the same through a clean cloth into a pint of grated pineapple; stir thoroughly and continuously until it commences to congeal. At this stage stir into it 1 pint of ice cream. Put all into a glass dish (ready for table) and set on ice. To be eaten with or without thick cream.

PINEAPPLE SPONGE.—*Miss H. J. Trumbull.*

1½ pint-can pineapple, 1 small cup sugar, ½ package gelatine, 1½ cups water, whites of 4 eggs. Soak the gelatine 2 hours in ½ a cup of water.

LIGHT DESSERTS.

Put the juice of the pineapple in a saucepan with the sugar and the remainder of the water; simmer 10 minutes; add the gelatine, take from the fire immediately, and strain into a tin basin. Add the chopped pineapple, and when partially cooled, add the beaten whites of the eggs, and beat until the mixture begins to thicken. Pour into a mold, and set away to harden. Serve with a soft custard made as follows:

CUSTARD SAUCE.—2 cups of milk, yolks of 4 eggs, 1 small cup of sugar. Heat the milk almost to boiling, add beaten yolks and sugar; stir constantly until it begins to thicken. Remove from the fire and add vanilla flavoring; allow it to cool, and when ready to serve, turn the pineapple sponge into a dish, and pour the custard around the base.

SPANISH CREAM.—*Mrs. D. Whittemore.*

1 quart of milk, yolks of 3 eggs, ½ package Knox's gelatine, 2 tablespoons of sugar; flavor with vanilla or lemon. Soak the gelatine 2 minutes in cold water. Beat the yolks and sugar together, add to the scalding milk, heat to boiling point, and add the gelatine, stirring all the time till it is dissolved. Pour into a mold and set on ice.

STRAWBERRY CROQUANTE.—*Mrs. J. L. Tharp.*

Dissolve 2 tablespoons of gelatine. Dip a mold in ice water; have large firm ripe strawberries; dip each berry in gelatine, and arrange around the sides and bottom of the mold. When cold, fill with whipped cream, and set on ice to harden.

NARCISSUS BLANC MANGE.—*Mrs. W. F. Jones.*

½ box of Knox's gelatine soaked in 1 teacup of cold water; when dissolved pour over it 1 pint of scalded milk; add ¾ cup of sugar and the beaten yolks of 2 eggs. Set away, and when it begins to set around the edges, transfer a spoonful at a time to another dish, and beat with an egg whip. Then flavor, and add 1 cup of whipped cream. Turn into a funnel-shaped mold. I use an old-fashioned scalloped cake pan with a funnel. Serve with whipped cream around the edge and in the funnel. If short of cream beat the 2 whites, sweeten a little, and add to the cream.

WINE JELLY.—*Miss H. Pregge.*

Soak 1 box gelatine in ½ pint of cold water 2 hours; then pour on 1½ pints boiling water, and stir until all is dissolved, but do not set it near the fire. Now add the juice of 2 lemons and sweeten to your taste. Wring a piece of thin muslin out of hot water, and lay in a fine strainer; strain the jelly through this after adding 1 pint of sherry wine to it. Make this jelly the day before you want to use it.

COFFEE JELLY.—*Miss Parsons, Tamalpais.*

3 pints cold coffee (such as is used at breakfast), 1 ounce gelatine. Boil 5 to 10 minutes. Set away in a mold after straining through a bag. Serve with sugar and cream. This makes 1 quart.

COFFEE PUDDING.—*Mrs. J. E. Alexander.*

1 pint of cream whipped light, ½ package gelatine dissolved in 1 cup milk, 1 large cup of strong coffee, 1 cup sugar, whites of 2 eggs. Add

the sugar and gelatine to the boiling coffee, strain and let cool; when the gelatine is cold, whip it slowly into the beaten whites until it is a firm froth, then add the whipped cream. Mold, and serve with cream.

CHARLOTTE RUSSE.—*Mrs. J. E. Alexander.*

1 pint of cream whipped light, 1 ounce gelatine dissolved in 1 gill of hot milk, whites of 2 eggs beaten to a stiff froth, 1 small teacup powdered sugar, flavor with ½ teaspoon bitter almonds and 1 teaspoon vanilla. Mix the cream, eggs, sugar and flavoring; add to it the gelatine and milk when nearly cold. Line a mold with lady fingers, fill with the mixture. Set on ice to cool.

ORANGE GELATINE.—*Mrs W. F. Jones.*

Pare 6 oranges, cut in thin slices (rejecting the seeds), and lay in a glass dish; dissolve ½ box of Knox's gelatine in 1 cup of cold water; when dissolved pour over it 1 pint or 2 cups of boiling water, 1 cup of white sugar, and strain upon the oranges. Serve with whipped cream or cream and sugar. To make variety cut in ½ dozen bananas and a can of sliced pineapple cut into small pieces. To double the recipe for the jelly, use the juice of the pineapple and have 2 quarts of jelly instead of one.

ORANGE WHIP.—*Miss Tena Bremner.*

Allow 1 quart of thick, rich cream to 6 oranges; make very sweet, and whip. Separate the oranges into sections; cut them in dice, taking out all membrane, leaving soft bits of pulp. Fill a glass dish with alternate layers of whipped cream and pulp, making upper layer of cream. Sprinkle top with macaroon crumbs.

ORANGE BASKETS.—*Mrs. W. F. Jones.*

Cut as many oranges as required, leaving half the peel whole for the baskets, and a strip across half an inch wide for the handle, that is, cut out 2 right-angled pieces each side of handle. Remove the pulp and juice, and use the juice for the orange jelly. Place the baskets in a pan with broken ice between to hold them upright. When ready to serve, put a teaspoon of whipped cream on top of each, and serve on orange leaves. It is an improvement to tie a small bow of ribbon on the center of the handle. To each pint of juice dissolve ½ box of Knox's gelatine in ½ cup of cold water. When dissolved, pour over the gelatine 1 cup of boiling water, 1 cup of sugar, the juice of 1 lemon, and then the fruit juice; strain through a cloth and fill the baskets.

CHOCOLATE CREAM PUDDING.—*Miss Margaret Bremner.*

1½ pints milk, ¾ cup sugar, 1½ squares sweetened chocolate, 5 level tablespoons corn starch, ¼ teaspoon salt, whites of 3 eggs. Boil milk, sugar, and grated chocolate together; then add the corn starch dissolved in a little cold milk; boil for 5 minutes, stirring constantly; then add the whites beaten to a stiff froth, and let boil 1 minute longer, stirring until done; put in a mold or molds as desired; serve cold with cream or whipped cream.

LIGHT DESSERTS.

RUSSIAN CREAM.—*Mrs. W. F. Jones*

Dissolve ½ box of Knox's gelatine in a little cold water, and when soft cook 20 minutes in 1 quart of milk; add 1 cup of sugar, remove to back of stove, and add the yolks of 4 eggs. When cool add the whites beaten stiff, and flavor to taste. Turn into a mold wet with cold water. Serve with whipped cream.

STRAWBERRY PUDDING.—*Mrs. W. F. Jones.*

1 box of Knox's gelatine dissolved in 1 quart of milk; set it on stove and let it gradually heat until the gelatine is thoroughly dissolved. Use 1 drawer of strawberries, reserving the best for a garnish; strain the rest through a cloth, add to the milk, and sweeten to taste. There should be about 2 quarts. Set away in mold to cool; when it begins to set, stir in 1 cup of 'cream whipped. When stiff, turn on to platter or any flat dish, put whipped cream all around, and drop the large reserved berries into the cream around the dish. Delicious.

Suits to
Order.

Gents' Furnishing
Goods.

Louis Becker

Merchant Tailor

Ladies' Tailor-made suits a Specialty. Fine stock of Suitings always on hand.

GIESKE BLOCK, B ST., NEAR SECOND,
San Rafael.

DRY GOODS, NOTIONS AND LADIES' SUNDRIES.

Jno. Wolfe

San Rafael, Cal.

DRUGGIST

Prescriptions carefully and accurately compounded. A complete stock of Drugs, chemicals and patent medicines.

Opera House Block

TOILET AND FANCY ARTICLES
AND PERFUMERY.

None but the Best at WOLFE'S.

R. M. Donne   H. J. Koch

R. M. DONNE & CO.

(Successors to Jossa & DuBois)

Toys, Cutlery, Cigars, Tobacco, School Supplies, Fishing Tackle, Etc.

Fine Stationery, Books and Periodicals

AGENCY FOR
All Morning and Evening Papers.

P. O. Box 674

Hay, Flour, Grain, Coal

Orders by mail or Telephone promptly attended to . . . .

Telephone Black 71.   **Storage and Commission.**

Frozen Dainties.

VANILLA CREAM.—*Mrs. Arthur Crosby.*

To a 1-gallon freezer, take the well beaten whites of 12 eggs, and equal parts of rich milk and cream, about 1 quart of each; add 1 tablespoon vanilla and 1 coffee cup of sugar. Taste, and if necessary add more sugar or extract. The freezer should be a little over ¾ full before freezing.

STRAWBERRY ICE CREAM.—*Mrs. Geo. Dodge.*

Hull 1 quart of berries, sprinkle with about 2 cups of sugar, and mash them. Let stand until the sugar is dissolved, and then squeeze through a cloth. Add 1 quart of cream, and if not sweet enough add more sugar. The pulp left in the cloth should be stirred into a little milk and squeezed again, in order to get all the berries but the seeds. Then freeze. Raspberry cream does not require so much of the fruit juice, as the flavor is stronger and richer.

ICE CREAM.—*Miss H. Pregge.*

1 quart milk, ⅓ box gelatine, 1 coffee cup sugar, 1 pint cream, flavor to taste. Put the gelatine and milk in a double boiler, and let it dissolve; then add sugar, cream and flavoring, and freeze.

TUTTI-FRUTTI ICE CREAM.—*Hoover.*

2 quarts sweet cream, 6 ounces dry granulated sugar, 8 ounces chopped glaced fruit, 1 teaspoon extract of vanilla: mix thoroughly together and freeze.

FRUIT ICE CREAM.—*Mrs. J. L. Tharp.*

1 quart peaches, bananas, or berries, or a grated pineapple (1 quart peaches preferred): pass through a colander. 1 cup water, 2 cups sugar, whites of 3 eggs beaten stiff; mix and freeze.

COFFEE FRAPPE.—*Mrs. D. Whittemore.*

1 quart rich cream, 2 cups white sugar, 1 cup strong black coffee. Freeze the same as ice cream.

MOUSSE.—*Mrs. W. F. Jones.*

Whip 1 quart of rich cream and add to the whites of 6 eggs beaten very stiff. Sweeten and flavor with vanilla to taste; put in mold and pack in ice and salt for 5 or 6 hours. If the cream is not rich enough to whip thick, whip it to a froth and keep skimming off the froth and put into a colander set in a bowl. Whip also that which drains into the bowl. When all is foamy, sweeten and flavor, and pack as above, omitting the eggs.

GOLDEN MOUSSE.—*Miss H. J. Trumbull.*

1 pint of cream before it is beaten; 5 eggs, yolks only, beaten stiff; 6 tablespoons of powdered sugar; 1 teaspoon of vanilla. Mix eggs, sugar and vanilla together; add all to the cream; put into a can packed in salt and ice, and let stand for 3 hours.

NESSELRODE PUDDING.—*Mrs. J. E. Alexander.*

1 pint of cream, 2 cups milk, 1 cup of sugar, 3 eggs, 1 tablespoon of vanilla, and a pinch of salt, 6 stale macaroons rolled fine. 12 candied cherries cut in quarters and soaked in ¼ cup sherry, ½ cup of nut meats (English walnuts, pecans, or hickory nuts), and a little citron. Scald the milk and cream, add the beaten yolks of the eggs, with sugar and salt. Let cool and flavor. Freeze, and when nearly frozen, add the beaten whites of the eggs, fruit and chopped nuts.

ROMAN PUNCH.—*Mrs. C. F. Robinson.*

Juice of ½ dozen lemons or 1 dozen limes; juice of 1 can of grated pineapple; 1 cup cold water; white of 1 egg beaten slightly; a wineglass of Jamaica rum; 1½ cups white sugar. If not sweet enough to suit, add more sugar and freeze rapidly to make it creamy. To be served before the game course.

PINEAPPLE SHERBET.—*Mrs. W. F. Jones.*

1 pint of fresh, or 1 can of grated pineapple; 1 pint of white sugar; 1 tablespoon of gelatine soaked in a little cold water; juice of 1 lemon. Pour 1 pint of boiling water over this mixture, and when well dissolved, strain through a cloth and freeze. Turn the freezer rapidly and continuously, to insure the sherbet being smooth and creamy.

ORANGE SHERBET.—*Mrs. J. M. Dollar.*

Soak 1 heaping tablespoon of Knox's gelatine in ½ cup cold water 10 minutes; add ½ cup boiling water; when dissolved, add 1 cup of sugar, 1 cup cold water, and 1 pint orange juice; when sugar is dissolved, strain and freeze.

You will never learn to Cook

unless you buy your

FUEL

from

S. H. Cheda & Co.

Yard and office, Fourth St., opposite Court House.

Telephone Red 14.

Telephone Red 81. San Rafael.

DOWNING & SONS

Wholesale and Retail Dealers in

Wood, Coal, Hay, Grain,

Corner
FOURTH ST. and TAMALPAIS AVE.
Opp. Broad Gauge Depot

Feed of all Kinds.
Charcoal, Coke and Kindling.

J. T. Cochrane P. H. Cochrane

COCHRANE BROS.

Practical **Horseshoers.**

Cor. C and Third Streets.
Adjoining Murray's Livery Stable.

Particular Attention given to Interfering, Overreaching, Corns and Quartercracks

Cakes, Cookies, Doughnuts
Etc.

Rules for Cake.

Sift cream of tartar, baking powder and soda dry with the flour.

Never dissolve soda in a liquid as it is almost sure to leave streaks, and after it is dissolved the mixture cannot be as light as when fermentation takes place in the dough.

When soda and sour milk are used always add a little baking powder, and the mixture will be far lighter and will not taste of soda as it is almost sure to do if sufficient soda is used to make very light.

Beat eggs separately.

Dredge fruit with flour to prevent its sinking, and always add it last.

Bake cake slowly at first, increasing the heat of the oven when well risen. Layer and sponge cakes require a quicker oven than loaf or fruit cake. Sponge ginger bread requires a slow oven. Cookies require a quick oven.

WEDDING CAKE.—*Mrs. Daniel Bradford.*

(This cake was used at Mrs. Bradford's wedding many years ago.)

5 pounds of flour, 5 pounds of sugar, 5 pounds of butter, 5 pounds of raisins, 5 pounds of citron, 10 pounds of currants, ½ pint of molasses, ½ pint of brandy, 35 eggs, 1½ ounces of mace, 1½ ounces of cinnamon, the same of cloves, 2 ounces of nutmeg, 1 teaspoon of soda.

FRUIT CAKE.—*Mrs. Robert Dollar.*

Flour 1 pound sifted and browned, butter 1 pound, sugar 1 pound, eggs 10, soda 1 teaspoon, raisins 1 pound, currants 1 pound, citron ½ pound, orange 2 ounces, lemon 2 ounces, almonds ½ pound, walnuts ½ pound, cinnamon 1 teaspoon, mace 1 teaspoon, cloves 1 teaspoon, allspice 1 teaspoon.

BLACK WEDDING CAKE.—*Mrs. L. A. Lancel.*

1 pound powdered sugar, 1 pound butter, 1 pound flour, 12 eggs, 1 pound raisins seeded and chopped, 1 pound currants washed and dredged, ½ pound citron cut into slips, 1 tablespoon cinnamon, 2 teaspoons nutmeg, 1 teaspoon cloves, 1 pint brandy. Cream the butter and sugar, add the beaten yolks, stir well; add the flour, then the spice, then the whipped whites with the flour; lastly the brandy. This quantity makes 2 large cakes; bake at least 2 hours in deep well buttered tins; test the cakes well, and be sure they are well done before taking them from the oven; put on icing.

FRUIT CAKE.—*Mrs. W. F. Jones.*

1 pound of butter, 1 pound of brown sugar, 1 pound of flour, 10 eggs, 2 pounds of raisins stoned and chopped, 2 pounds of currants washed carefully and dried, 1 pound of citron sliced fine, 1 teacup of syrup, 1 teacup of brandy, 2 nutmegs, 1 small bottle of lemon extract, 2 tablespoons of cinnamon, 1 tablespoon of cloves, 4 teaspoons yeast powder, and 1 tablespoon of sugar burned and dissolved in a tablespoon of water. Stir butter and sugar to a cream, then add eggs well beaten, syrup, brandy, lemon, spices, and the fruit dredged with some of the flour. This will make a large and a small loaf. The large loaf should bake about 3 hours in a slow oven.

FRUIT CAKE.—*Mrs. W. J. Dickson.*

1 pound of sugar, 1 pound of butter, 1 pound of flour, 10 eggs, 4 pounds fruit (raisins, currants and citron), 1 wine glass of wine (sherry) or brandy, 1 cup of syrup, 1 teaspoon mace, cinnamon and cloves. Beat the butter and sugar to a cream with the hand; stir in the eggs, 1 at a time, beating well with the hand, after which add the syrup, wine and spices, then the fruit, and lastly the flour. Bake 1½ hours in tins lined with buttered paper.

MRS. HOAG'S WEDDING CAKE.—*Mrs. Sawyer.*

1½ pounds sugar, 1½ pounds flour, 1 pound butter, 3 pounds raisins, 2¼ pounds currants, 1½ pounds citron, 10 eggs, 2 wine glasses brandy, 2 glasses wine, 1 cup cold coffee, 1 tablespoon soda, 2 tablespoons cloves, 1 tablespoon mace, 1 tablespoon allspice, 1 tablespoon cinnamon, and a nutmeg. Bake 4 hours. If you choose, brown part of the flour.

PLAIN FRUIT CAKE.—*Mrs. C. F. Robinson*

1 cup butter, 3 cups brown sugar, 1 cup molasses, 1 cup sweet milk, 6¼ cups flour, 2 teaspoons soda and 2 of baking powder, 5 eggs, 1 teaspoon each of cinnamon and cloves, 1 nutmeg, 1 pound currants, 2 pounds of raisins. Bake slowly 3 hours.

QUEEN'S CAKE.—*Mrs. E. R. Donohoe.*

1 pound of sugar, ¾ pound of butter, 1 pound of flour, 6 eggs, 1 gill of wine, 1 gill of brandy, 1 gill of sweet cream, 1 nutmeg; all simmered together; raisins and citron to taste.

MEASURE CAKE.—*Mrs. E. R. Donohoe.*

3 cups brown sugar, 2 cups butter, 1 cup sour cream, 5 cups flour, 5 eggs, 1 teaspoon saleratus; brandy, wine, fruit and spice to taste.

GENERAL GORDON CAKE.—*Mrs. J. L. Tharp.*

¾ pound butter and 1 pound sugar creamed well together; break in 1 egg at a time until you have used 10; beat well, and add a paper of cornstarch; add 1 teaspoon of yeast powder; flavor with vanilla. Bake quickly.

CIDER CAKE.—*Mrs. Daniel Bradford.*

6 cups of flour, 4 cups of sugar, 2 cups of butter, 2 cups of cider, 5

eggs, 2 teaspoons of soda in the cider, 2 nutmegs, 2 large spoons of cinnamon, same of cloves; cider added last.

A RICH SEED CAKE.

Mix into ¾ pound butter beaten to a cream, 1 pound flour, 1 pound sifted sugar, ¼ pound sweet almonds blanched and cut, 1 piece each candied orange, lemon and citron peel also cut to taste, a little ground cinnamon and mace, some caraway seeds, and 8 eggs well beaten. Pour into a tin nicely lined with buttered paper; sprinkle some caraway seeds on the top, and bake in a moderate oven.

MRS. RADER'S CAKE.—*Mrs McMahon.*

1 cup butter, 2 cups sugar, 2 cups flour, ½ cup milk, ½ cup chocolate, good measure, 1 cup chopped walnuts, 4 eggs, 1 cup mashed potatoes. 2 teaspoons baking powder, 1 teaspoon each of cloves, cinnamon and nutmeg. Bake slowly. Delicious.

MARSHMALLOW CAKE.—*Mrs. A. A. Smith.*

1 cup powdered sugar, 5 tablespoons butter, 1 cup milk, the whites 4 eggs, 2 cups flour, 2 teaspoons baking powder. Frost the cake; then split marshmallows and place on the top of the frosting. Flavor with lemon.

HONEYMOON CAKE.—*Mrs. Daniel Bradford.*

10 cups of flour, 6 cups of sugar, 3 cups of butter, 6 eggs, nearly 3 cups of milk, 1 teaspoon of soda, nutmeg or lemon; and fruit if liked.

LOAF CAKE.—*Mrs. Daniel Bradford.*

3 cups of light bread dough, 2 cups of sugar, 1 cup of butter (not heaping), nutmeg and cinnamon, 2 eggs, 1 teaspoon of soda in 1 teaspoon of milk; a little wine or brandy. Bake soon as mixed.

BREAD CAKE.—*Mrs. McMahon.*

1 cup loaf dough, 2 cups sugar, 1 cup butter, 3 eggs, 1 teaspoon soda, 2 tablespoons sweet milk, ½ cup currants, nutmeg and cloves. Beat yolks very light, cream butter and sugar, add spice, milk, soda, and dough. Stir all until well mixed. Put in the beaten whites, lastly the fruit. Beat the mixture 5 minutes. Let rise 20 minutes, and bake.

ANGEL CAKE.—*Mrs. W. G. Corbaley.*

Sift 1 cup flour 6 times, then add 1 teaspoon cream of tartar, and sift 4 times. Sift 1½ cups granulated sugar 6 times. Beat the whites of 12 eggs very stiff; add 1 teaspoon vanilla, and gently stir into the flour and sugar. Pour into a perfectly dry, ungreased pan with a funnel. Bake 45 minutes in a moderate oven; on taking from the oven turn the pan upside down, putting 2 sticks under the edge of each side of the pan to permit circulation of air. When cold remove from the pan.

DEVIL'S FOOD CAKE.—*Lulu Stuart.*

1 cup brown sugar, ½ cup butter, ½ cup sweet milk, yolks of 3 eggs, 1 cup sweet chocolate, 2½ cups flour, and 2 teaspoons baking powder. Beat the sugar, butter and eggs; then heat the chocolate and milk;

CAKES, COOKIES, DOUGHNUTS, ETC.

when cool, add it to the cake; then add flour and baking powder; bake in 3 layers.

TEA CAKE.—*Miss H. Pregge.*

½ cup butter, 1½ cups white sugar, 2 eggs, 1 cup milk, 2 teaspoons cream of tartar, 1 teaspoon soda, 3 cups flour, ⅓ of a nutmeg, 1 teaspoon cloves, 1 teaspoon cinnamon, 1 cup stoned raisins.

SPOTTED CAKE.—*Mrs. W. J. Dickson.*

For the white layer mix the whites of 4 eggs, 1 cup white sugar, ⅔ cup butter, ⅔ cup milk, 2 teaspoons baking powder, and flour enough to make a thick batter. For the dark layer mix the yolks of 4 eggs, 1 cup brown sugar, ½ cup molasses, ⅔ cup butter, ⅔ cup milk, 2 teaspoons baking powder, 1 teaspoon each of cloves, cinnamon and nutmeg; 1 cup raisins chopped fine, and flour enough to make a thick batter. Put a spoonful of the light and dark layers alternately into the cake pan, and bake.

DELICATE CAKE.—*Mrs. W. J. Lickson.*

1 cup sugar, ½ cup butter, 2 eggs, ½ cup milk, 1½ cups flour, 2 teaspoons baking powder.

POUND CAKE.—*Mrs. W. F. Jones.*

1 pound of flour, 1 pound of sugar, ¾ pound of butter, 12 eggs, 2 heaping teaspoons of baking powder, 2 teaspoons extract of lemon or vanilla; cream the butter, and add the flour; beat the yolks, and add the sugar. Whip the whites to a stiff froth and add this and the yolks gradually to the flour; add the baking powder mixed with a little flour, and then the extract. Bake in moderate oven.

FIG CAKE.—*Lulu Stuart.*

White part: 2 cups granulated sugar, ½ cup butter, whites of 5 eggs well beaten, ⅔ cup sweet milk, 2 cups flour, 2 teaspoons baking powder. Dark part: 1 cup brown sugar, butter the size of a walnut, 1 cup chopped figs, ½ cup milk, 1 egg, 1 cup flour, 1 teaspoon baking powder. Bake the cake in 3 layers, putting the dark one in the center. Frost if desired.

SPICE CAKE.—*Mrs. E. B. Mahon.*

Yolks of 5 eggs, 2 cups of brown sugar, ½ pound of butter, 1 cup of sour cream, 2½ pounds of flour, 1 teaspoon of soda, 2 of cloves, 3 of cinnamon, 3 of allspice, 3 of ginger, 1 nutmeg; bake same as jelly cake; put icing between, made of the whites of the eggs.

WATERMELON CAKE.—*Mrs. E. B. Mahon*

Whites of 3 eggs, 1 cup white sugar, ½ cup butter, ½ cup sweet milk, 2 even cups flour, 1 teaspoon yeast powder; flavor with lemon or vanilla. For red part: take the white of 1 egg and the yolks of the others; beat to a stiff froth; add ½ cup red sugar, ¼ cup butter, ¼ cup milk, 1 cup flour, and 1 teaspoon yeast powder. Take ½ of the white mixture for the bottom layer; then add red mixture; lay on 2 rows of seeded raisins so they will be an inch apart, then add the rest of the white for the top layer; bake in a loaf tin.

WALNUT CAKE.—*Mrs. Arthur Crosby.*

1½ cups granulated sugar, ¾ cup butter, ½ cup milk, 2¾ cups flour, whites of 5 eggs, 3 teaspoons yeast powder, 1 teaspoon vanilla, 1 pound walnuts before they are shelled. Cream the butter and sugar, add the flour, milk and eggs alternately; add the yeast powder with the last of the flour, and dredge the nuts with flour. Chop half of the nuts, and put inside, reserving the halves that are not broken to put on the top of the cake after frosting. Bake in a sheet tin; have the cake about 1 inch thick before baking.

CUP CAKE.—*Mrs. W. F. Jones.*

1 cup of butter creamed with 2 cups of sugar, 1 cup of milk, 6 eggs, 4 cups of flour sifted with 3 teaspoons baking powder.

BRIDE'S CAKE.—*Mrs. W. F. Jones.*

4 cups sugar, 2 cups butter, 2 cups milk, 6 teaspoons baking powder, 7 cups flour, whites of 20 eggs. Cream butter and sugar together; then slowly add the milk, flour and whites of eggs, stirring constantly; add baking powder in the last cup of flour. Bake 3 hours. ½ of this recipe makes a large cake, and is always nice if stirred sufficiently and if the oven is right.

LADY CAKE.—*Mrs. Daniel Bradford.*

2 coffee cups of sugar and 2 tablespoons of butter (not heaping) rubbed to a cream; 1 teacup of milk, or sour cream; ½ teaspoon of soda in the milk, 2 coffee cups of flour, whites of 8 eggs, and the grated rind and the juice of 1 lemon.

VELVET CAKE.—*Mrs. C. F. Robinson.*

1½ cups powdered sugar, ½ cup butter creamed; yolks of 3 eggs broken into this and beaten well; ½ cup water, ½ cup corn starch, 1½ cups flour, 2 level teaspoons baking powder; then add the whites of eggs beaten stiff, and flavor to taste. Bake in a long tin.

SILVER CAKE.—*Mrs. Fred Sawyer.*

½ cup butter, 1½ cups sugar, 2 cups flour, ½ cup milk, the whites of 6 eggs, 1 teaspoon cream tartar, ½ teaspoon soda. Cream butter and sugar, beat the whites to a stiff paste, add the rest of the ingredients a little at a time, reserving a little milk in a cup in which put cream tartar and soda, and add to the cake last; flavor to taste, and bake in a moderate oven.

SHORTBREAD.

Put into a bowl 1 pound flour, ¼ pound rice flour, and ½ pound brown sugar; mix well together and pour in ¾ pound butter already melted in a saucepan, using a clean wooden spoon to stir the ingredients together. Divide into 6 cakes, and knead out quickly on the board with the hand, using rice flour to dust the board and hands. Prick with a fork all over, and slip a square of paper under each cake as it is done; put on a baking sheet and bake in a moderate oven until a delicate brown. The less kneading shortbread gets, the better; never roll it.

SCOTCH SHORTCAKE.—*Mrs. J. M. Dollar.*

4 ounces white sugar, ½ pound slightly salted butter, 1 pound of flour. Mix the flour and butter with the hands, then add the sugar, and work all into a smooth ball, then roll out until it is an inch thick; prick over with a fork, cut into squares, prick around the edges, and bake for ½ an hour in an oven with a moderate fire. Caraway seed candies are nice sprinkled on the top before putting in the oven.

SPONGE CAKE.—*Mrs. A. E. Menzies.*

8 eggs, 1 pound sugar, ½ pound of flour, the grated rind of 1 lemon, the juice of ½ a lemon. Beat the whites and yolks separately. Mix together yolks, sugar and lemon; when well mixed stir in the whites; mix in the flour very gently.

SPONGE CAKE.—*Mrs. Oliver.*

6 eggs, 1 cup powdered sugar, 1 cup flour, 1 level teaspoon baking powder, a pinch of salt. Beat the yolks and sugar to a cream; then beat the whites thoroughly; beat 1 tablespoon of the whites and the flour alternately into each other; put the salt and baking powder into the last tablespoon of flour.

WINTER SPONGE CAKE.—*Mrs. J. M. Dollar.*

4 eggs, 2 cups sugar, 2 cups flour, 2 teaspoons baking powder, 1 cup boiling water, 1 teaspoon lemon or vanilla flavoring, a pinch of salt. Beat the eggs and sugar together; add flour, baking powder and flavoring; lastly add the boiling water, stirring all the time; this will be rather thin but is delicious. It can be frosted with any kind of frosting.

GOLDEN LETTERS.—*Mrs. W. B. Bradford.*

Bake small round sponge cakes, and when the frosting is on and hard, dip a small brush in the beaten yolk of 1 egg, and write a word or name on top.

DOMINOES.—*Mrs. W. B. Bradford.*

Bake sponge cake in thin sheets, and cut into oblong pieces the shape of a domino. Frost the top and sides, and when hard, make the lines and dots with a small brush dipped in melted chocolate. Both of these recipes make pretty cakes for children's parties.

SPONGE CAKE OR LADY FINGERS.—*Mrs. W. F Jones.*

1 cup of sugar and the yolks of 4 eggs beaten to a cream; 1 tablespoon cold water or juice of ½ lemon; 1 cup flour sifted with 1 teaspoon baking powder; the whites of eggs added last, beaten to a stiff froth; flavor to taste if you use water. This can be pinched through a conical shaped paper into lady fingers, or baked in a loaf. For lady fingers, bake them on paper on a pan upside down. When baked, pour some cold water over the drain, and lay the paper on this damp place. As soon as the lady fingers loosen, remove from paper and place 2 together.

ICE CREAM CAKE.—*Mrs. W. F. Jones.*

Bake the above sponge cake in 3 layers or in muffin rings, and split them when baked.

CAKES, COOKIES, DOUGHNUTS, ETC.

FILLING.—Whip 1 pint of cream and add about ½ cup of sugar or to taste; flavor with vanilla. Take 1 pound of almonds, shell, blanch, and chop very fine, and stir into the cream, reserving some of the blanched almonds whole to put on top. Make soft frosting of the whites of 2 eggs and 4 tablespoons sugar; put the almonds on top.

JELLY ROLL.—*Mrs. Geo. Bunn.*

2 eggs, ½ cup sugar, ½ cup flour, less than ½ teaspoon baking powder. Bake in a quick oven; turn out upon a cloth, spread with jelly and roll while warm.

WHIPPED CREAM CAKE.—*Mrs. D. Whittemore.*

1 cup powdered sugar, 3 eggs (yolks and whites beaten separately), 1½ cups sifted flour, 3 large spoons cold water, melted butter the size of a walnut; beat well five minutes. Bake in jelly tins (three layers); when cold, fill with ½ pint cream whipped; frost with soft frosting; flavor with vanilla.

CREAM CAKE.—*Mrs. E. B. Mahon.*

Beat 2 eggs and 1 cup sugar thoroughly; add 3 tablespoons cold water, 1½ cups flour, 1 teaspoon yeast powder. When baked, split and put in the cream, made as follows: 1 pint milk, 2 tablespoons corn starch, 1 beaten egg, sugar to sweeten; add a small piece of butter; flavor to suit; stir while cooking.

JAM CAKE.—*Mrs. McMahon.*

3 eggs, 1 cup sugar, ¾ cup butter, 1 cup jam (wild blackberry is best), 2 cups flour, 1 teaspoon soda, 1 teaspoon yeast powder, 3 teaspoons sweet milk or cream, 1 teaspoon cloves, 1 teaspoon cinnamon, ½ of 1 nutmeg; bake in layers, and put together with boiled icing or with whipped cream.

SPICED FIG CAKE.—*Mrs. A. A. Smith.*

Cream ½ cup of butter with ½ cup of white sugar and ½ cup of brown sugar; add the yolks of 4 eggs beaten light and mixed with ½ cup of cold water, 3 tablespoons of grated chocolate, 1 teaspoon each of allspice and cinnamon, and ¼ teaspoon of cloves; the whites of 4 eggs well beaten should be added just before the last of the flour, and 2 teaspoons of baking powder.

FILLING FOR THIS CAKE.—½ pound of figs chopped, and boiled in ½ cup of water till tender; then add 1 scant cup of sugar and the juice of 1 lemon; boil till it is thick like jelly, and spread between layers.

CHOCOLATE LAYER CAKE.—*Mrs. A. A. Smith.*

The whites of 3 eggs, 2 cups of sugar, 1 cup of sweet milk, 2 large tablespoons of butter, 3 cups of flour, 2 heaping teaspoons of baking powder. Bake half the batter in 2 pans, and add ½ cup of grated chocolate to the remainder, making 2 layers. When baked, pile up alternately dark and light, with chocolate filling between.

MARSHMALLOW CAKE.—*Mrs. McMahon.*

1 cup butter, 2 cups sugar, 1 cup milk, yolks of 4 eggs, whites of 3

eggs, 1 teaspoon vanilla, 4 cups flour, 3 rounded teaspoons baking powder; bake in layers. For the filling, put ½ pound of marshmallows on an agate dish, and place in oven until they have melted and run together. Make a boiled icing with 1 cup of granulated sugar and ⅓ of a cup of hot water boiled together until the syrup hisses; then pour it over the stiffly beaten white of 1 egg; add the melted marshmallows, and beat slowly 5 minutes. Spread this between the layers and on top.

LEMON CHEESE CAKE.—*Miss A. Gordon.*

2 cups sugar, ½ cup butter, ¾ cup sweet milk, whites of 6 eggs, 3 cups flour, 3 teaspoons baking powder: bake in jelly cake tins.

SAUCE FOR THE SAME.—Grated rind and juice of 2 lemons, yolks of 3 eggs, ½ cup butter, 1 cup sugar; mix all together, set on stove, and cook till thick as sponge, stirring all the time; then use like jelly between the cakes.

ORANGE CAKE.—*Mrs. Hoyt.*

2½ cups flour, ½ cup butter, 2 eggs, 1 cup sugar, 1½ teaspoons yeast powder, ¾ cup milk. Bake.

FILLING.—1 cup sugar, 1 cup boiling water; let boil together; add 1 large cooking spoon corn starch (wet up), the grated rind and juice of 2 oranges and 1 lemon; cook until stiff; after cooling, put it between the layers of cake.

LAYER CAKE.—*Mrs. W. F. Jones.*

1 cup of sugar rubbed with ½ cup of butter, ½ cup of milk, any extract, 3 eggs, 1½ cups of flour sifted with 1 teaspoon baking powder. Bake in 3 layers.

LEMON FILLING.—1 tablespoon corn starch wet in a little cold water; pour over this about 1 cup of boiling water, 1 tablespoon butter, ¾ cup of sugar, the grated rind and juice of 1 lemon, and the yolks of 2 eggs.

SOFT FROSTING.—Beat the whites of the 2 eggs very stiff, and gently sift in 4 heaping tablespoons of powdered sugar.

MINNE-HA-HA CAKE.—*Mrs. W. F. Jones.*

Make the layer cake above, only instead of 3 eggs use the yelks of 6 eggs for the cake. Beat the whites very stiff, and add gently 12 rounded tablespoons of powdered sugar. Take ⅓ of the frosting and add to it 1 cup of stoned and chopped raisins for the first layer. Shell 1 pound of walnuts, reserve about 1 dozen halves for the top, chop the rest and add to a third of the frosting for the second layer. Put the balance of the frosting on top, and dot the halves over. Turtles made of raisins and cloves are an addition on top.

FILLING FOR NUT CAKE.—*Mrs. W. F. Jones.*

1 cup of milk, ½ cup of sugar, butter the size of a walnut, 2 teaspoons corn starch, yolks of 2 eggs, 1 cup of chopped walnuts. Spread while hot. Make soft frosting out of the whites of the eggs.

CREAM FOR CHOCOLATE CAKE.—1 cup sweet milk, 1 tablespoon butter, 1 cup sugar, 1 cup grated chocolate, 1 tablespoon corn starch, yolks of 2 eggs and 1 teaspoon vanilla. Make soft frosting of the whites.

BANANA FILLING.—Spread with whipped cream sweetened; over this put a layer of bananas cut round, with more whipped cream over the bananas. Soft frosting.

CARAMEL FILLING.—2 cups brown sugar, ⅓ cup butter, ⅓ cup milk. Brown the sugar, stirring constantly; then add butter, and lastly the milk. Cook until quite thick, so it will not run. Lastly add 1 teaspoon vanilla, and spread while hot between the layers and over the top of the cake.

COCOANUT FILLING.—For the cake part use the yolks of 6 eggs instead of 3 eggs. A fresh grated cocoanut is much nicer than any prepared cocoanut. Beat the whites of 6 eggs very stiff, and add 12 tablespoons of sugar. Spread a layer of frosting and sprinkle thick with cocoanut for the inside layers, reserving a good deal of frosting for the top and sides. When the frosting is well spread, sprinkle cocoanut over the top and throw it against the sides until the cake is well covered.

FROSTING.—*Mrs. A. A. Smith.*

When eggs are dear make cake frosting by boiling 3 tablespoons of milk; when cool, flavor and thicken with powdered sugar; make quite stiff, and beat until smooth and light; dip the knife in cold water when spreading.

BOILED ICING.—*Mrs. R E. Neil.*

Wet one cup of sugar with enough water to moisten; boil until it hairs from the spoon, and gradually pour it into the well beaten whites of 2 eggs.

CHOCOLATE ICING.—*Mrs. McMahon.*

Put into a shallow pan 4 tablespoons of powdered chocolate, and place it where it will melt slowly but not burn. When melted, stir in 3 tablespoons of milk or cream, and 1 of water; mix all well together; add 1 scant teacup sugar; boil 5 minutes; while still hot, and when the cakes are nearly cold, spread on evenly, and set in a warm oven to dry.

CHOCOLATE FROSTING.—*Mrs. J. M. Dollar.*

2 cups sugar, ½ cup grated chocolate, ½ cup sweet milk; boil all together for about 10 minutes; when done, add vanilla to taste, and stir until nearly cool, then spread on cake. This will cut nicely.

SOFT GINGER CAKE.—*Miss Parsons, Tamalpais.*

1 cup sugar, 1 cup butter, 1 cup boiling water, 1 cup New Orleans molasses, 2 eggs, 2 small teaspoons soda, 1 tablespoon ginger, flour to make a thick batter, or till it drops in plaits or folds from the spoon (more flour makes it too stiff). Excellent.

SYRUP CAKE.—*Mrs. Geo. Bunn.*

1 cup sour cream, 1 cup syrup, 1 teaspoon soda, 1 teaspoon ginger, 1 teaspoon cinnamon, sufficient flour to mix pretty stiff with a spoon. Bake in sheets; to be eaten hot. Eggs are not needed in this recipe.

SPONGE GINGERBREAD.—*Mrs. E. B. Mahon.*

2 eggs, 1 cup of sugar, 2 heaping tablespoons of butter, 1 cup of molasses, 1 cup of sour milk, 4½ cups of flour, 2 teaspoons of saleratus

(not soda) dissolved in hot water, 2 teaspoons of ginger, 1 teaspoon of cinnamon, 1 pound of seeded raisins, ½ pound of currants. Mix molasses, sugar, butter, and spices together; warm them slightly and beat until light; add the yolks when beaten, then the milk; then the flour and saleratus; beat well 5 minutes; bake in shallow pans.

GINGER CAKE.—*Mrs. E. B. Mahon.*

1 egg, 3 tablespoons of melted butter, ½ cup of syrup, ½ cup of brown sugar, scant ½ cup of milk, 1½ cups of flour, 1 teaspoon of ginger (more if liked), also cinnamon, and 1 teaspoon of yeast powder or soda.

SOFT GINGERBREAD.—*Mrs. A. A. Smith.*

1 cup New Orleans molasses, 1 teaspoon soda, 1 egg, 1 cup flour, 4 tablespoons of melted butter, 8 tablespoons of boiling water, 1 tablespoon of ginger. Mix quickly, and bake from 15 to 20 minutes in a hot oven.

GINGERBREAD COOKIES.—*Mrs. Daniel Bradford.*

1 cup molasses, 1 cup sugar, 1 cup of part lard and part butter, ½ cup of milk, and 1 teaspoon of soda; ginger; flour to roll out; to be mixed soft.

GINGER SNAPS.—*Mrs. W. F. Jones.*

2 cups of molasses, 1 cup of butter or lard, 1 level tablespoon soda, 2 level tablespoons ginger, a little cinnamon if liked; boil the syrup, butter and spices together, adding soda last when boiling; then remove from the fire and add about 1 quart of flour, or enough to roll. Endeavor to roll out without more flour; roll very thin, and bake in a moderate oven. When cool, pack away in tight cans to prevent getting soft.

GINGER SNAPS.—*Mrs. Wm. Alexander.*

2 cups molasses, 1 cup sugar, 1 cup melted butter or shortening. Let the above come to a boil, then add 2 teaspoons soda, 1 quart flour, 1 teaspoon ginger, 1 teaspoon cinnamon, ¼ teaspoon cloves, ½ teaspoon allspice, 1 teaspoon salt. Dissolve the soda, and pour it into the molasses; pour boiled molasses, sugar and shortening into the flour. Roll very thin.

GINGER SNAPS.—*Mrs. E. B. Mahon.*

2 eggs, ½ cup of brown sugar, ½ cup of syrup, a piece of butter and a little lard, ½ teaspoon of ginger, ½ teaspoon of soda, flour to suit; roll thin and bake slowly.

GINGER COOKIES.—*Mrs. A. A. Smith.*

1 cup of molasses, 1 cup of sugar, 1 cup of lard, 1 cup of boiling water, 1 tablespoon of ginger, 2 teaspoons of soda; ½ teaspoon each of allspice, cinnamon and cloves; roll thin, and bake in a quick oven.

MOLASSES JUMBLES.—*Mrs. McMahon.*

1 cup of sugar; butter size of an egg; mix to cream; add 1 cup of flour, and molasses enough to mix it. Drop in buttered pans and bake. When done and while hot, roll over a round stick the size of a broom handle.

HERMITS.—*Mrs. Geo. M. Dodge.*

1½ cups sugar, 1 cup butter, 3 eggs, 1 tablespoon sour cream, ¼ of a teaspoon soda dissolved in a very little boiling water, 1 teaspoon each of cinnamon and cloves, 1 cup chopped raisins, 1 cup chopped walnuts, and some citron if liked. Mix with sufficient flour to roll; cut out as cookies, and bake in a moderate oven. Excellent, and will keep some time.

HERMIT COOKIES.—*Mrs. W. G. Corbaley.*

1 cup of chopped raisins, 1 cup of butter, 1 cup of sugar, ½ cup of molasses, 2 eggs, 2 tablespoons sour milk, 1 teaspoon each of soda, cinnamon, cloves, and 1 nutmeg; flour to roll.

OATMEAL DATE COOKIES.—*Mrs. J. M. Dollar*

Take 1 quart fine oatmeal, 2 cups flour, 2 cups brown sugar, 2 eggs, ¾ cup of butter or other shortening, 3 teaspoons baking powder, a pinch of salt, and a little milk. Mix the oatmeal, flour, baking powder, salt and sugar all together, then add the butter; mix well. Add the eggs well beaten with just enough milk to make a stiff dough. Roll out half the quantity thin, have some dates stoned, and spread a layer on the dough; roll out the other half thin and lay on the top; roll it a little, cut in shapes, and bake in a moderate oven.

TEA CAKES OR COOKIES.—*Mrs. W. F. Jones.*

3 cups of sugar and 2 of butter worked to a cream; 3 eggs, 1 cup of sour milk, 1½ teaspoons soda (scant measure) sifted in with some flour, 1 tablespoon lemon juice or extract, and flour to roll out, but not too stiff. Take out a large spoonful at a time, roll very thin, then sprinkle over with sugar and a few caraway seeds. Run the rolling pin over again, cut out, and bake in a quick oven. Very nice.

SOFT COOKIES.—*Mrs. E. B. Mahon.*

1 egg, 1 cup of sugar, a piece of butter, ½ cup of sour milk, a few caraway seeds, 1½ cups of flour and ¼ teaspoon of saleratus.

COOKIES.—*Mrs. F. M. Angellotti.*

¾ cup of butter, 1 cup of sugar, 2 beaten eggs, 2 teaspoons of baking powder, 2 tablespoons milk; mix with enough flour to roll out.

SUGAR COOKIES WITHOUT EGGS.—*Mrs. Geo Bunn.*

1 cup butter, 2 cups sugar, 5 cups flour, a little nutmeg; 1 teaspoon soda and 2 teaspoons of cream of tartar. Roll out not too thin, and bake quickly.

COOKIES.—*Mrs. Hoyt.*

½ cup of butter, 1 cup of sugar, 1 tablespoon of milk, 2 eggs, 1 heaping teaspoon of yeast powder, flavor to taste; enough flour to roll out very thin.

BUTTER COOKIES.—*Mrs. Wm. Lichtenberg.*

1 pound of butter, 3 eggs, ¾ pound of sugar, 1 pound of flour, the juice of ½ lemon, and the grated rind. Stir the butter to a cream; add the sugar, eggs, and lemon gradually; after adding the flour, knead the dough, roll little balls, flatten them into cooky shape on the tin, making

a little hole with the finger in the middle. Bake in a moderately hot oven.

COOKIES.—*Mrs. E. B. Mahon.*

1 cup of butter, 3 eggs, 2 cups of sugar, ½ cup of milk, 2 teaspoons of yeast powder, a little nutmeg, and flour to suit.

COCOANUT COOKIES.—*Miss Lulu Stuart.*

1 cup cocoanut, 1 cup granulated sugar, 1 cup butter, ½ cup sour milk, 1 teaspoon soda, 1 egg, flour enough to roll thin; sprinkle with sugar, and bake in a quick oven.

CREAM CAKE.—*Miss H. J. Trumbull.*

1 scant cup white sugar, 2 eggs, 1 scant cup sweet cream, 1 oven cup of flour, a pinch of salt, and 1 teaspoon of baking powder. Break the eggs into a cake dish, put in the sugar, next the cream and salt, and lastly the flour with the baking powder sifted in; then beat it all together briskly 2 or 3 minutes. Excellent for layer, loaf or drop cakes.

WALNUT WAFERS.—*Mrs. W. Locke.*

1 cup of brown sugar, 1 cup of walnuts broken into small pieces, 2 eggs, a pinch of salt, 3 heaping tablespoons of flour. Drop on buttered tins, and bake in quick oven a few minutes.

PEANUT WAFERS.—*Mrs. J. E. Alexander.*

½ cup sugar, 2 rounded tablespoons butter, 2 eggs, 2 tablespoons milk, ¾ cup flour before it is sifted, 1 teaspoon of baking powder, 1 cup chopped peanuts, 1 teaspoon vanilla, pinch of salt. Drop from a teaspoon.

VIENNA CAKES.—*Mrs. Wm. Lichtenberg.*

½ pound of butter, ½ pound of sugar, ½ pound of flour, 4 eggs, ¼ pound of almonds, cinnamon. Melt the butter and use only the clear part, as the sediment will spoil the cake. Stir it until cool and thick; add the sugar, flour and eggs; spread the dough on the tin with a knife as thin as possible; chop the almonds and mix them with some sugar and cinnamon as a flavor, and strew this mixture over the top of the dough. Bake in a good hot oven; as soon as done take a large sharp knife and cut in small squares or any other desired shape.

CHOCOLATE NUT STRIPS.—*Mrs. McMahon.*

6 eggs, 2 cups of sugar, 5 sticks of chocolate (or a coffee cup of the grated chocolate), 1 pound of shelled almonds, 1 teaspoon cinnamon, 1 teaspoon cloves, 1 nutmeg grated, 1 teaspoon vanilla, 2 teaspoons baking powder, flour enough to roll out, and bake in sheets. When done cut in strips. Reserve the yolk of 1 egg, add a little water and sugar, and brush with a pastry brush before baking.

MACAROONS.—*Mrs. W. F. Jones.*

Take 1 pound of almonds, shell, and blanch in boiling water; wipe dry and chop very fine; then pound in a mortar, and add while pounding 1 tablespoon of rose water, or use other extracts if preferred. Beat the whites of 3 eggs very stiff; gently add ½ pound of powdered sugar, and then the almonds. When well mixed, drop from a teaspoon small parcels on baking tins rubbed with olive oil. Put them 2 inches apart, sift sugar over the top, and bake in rather a slow oven.

CHOCOLATE MACAROONS.—*Mrs. McMahon.*

Whites of 5 eggs beaten to a stiff froth, 1 pound white sugar, ½ teaspoon of cloves, cinnamon and allspice, 2 sticks of grated chocolate, 1 pound grated almonds; bake in a slow oven.

MACAROONS.—*Mrs. Wm. Lichtenberg.*

¼ pound sweet almonds, ¼ pound bitter almonds, ¾ pound sugar, 3 eggs, whites only. Grate the almonds, mix them with the whipped whites of eggs and the sugar. Drop a teaspoonful on cake paper, and bake in a moderate oven.

KISSES.—*Mrs. W. F. Jones.*

To the well beaten white of 1 egg gently sift in 1 heaping tablespoon of powdered sugar, 1 of granulated sugar and a few drops of vanilla extract. Drop on brown paper and bake very slowly.

CHOCOLATE KISSES.—*Mrs. W. F. Jones.*

To the white of an egg well beaten, gently stir in 1 heaping tablespoon of granulated sugar and the same of grated chocolate. Drop on brown paper and bake very slowly.

DOUGHNUTS.—*Mrs. F. M. Angellotti.*

1 cup of milk, and butter the size of an egg melted in; 3 eggs, 2 teaspoons baking powder, 1 cup of sugar, nutmeg, and enough flour to roll.

DOUGHNUTS.—*Mrs. W. Fraser.*

2½ cups white sugar, 3 eggs, 5 teaspoons melted butter, 3 teaspoons baking powder, 2 cups of sweet or sour milk; flavor with nutmeg, and add flour enough to roll out. Fry in hot lard to a light brown.

DOUGHNUTS.—*Mrs. W. F. Jones.*

3 eggs, 1 cup of sugar, ½ cup of sour milk, ½ cup of sour cream, a little nutmeg, and flour to roll. Sift in with the flour 1 teaspoon soda and a little baking powder. Fry in hot fat, drain from a fork and drop on brown paper as they come from the fat. Sprinkle with powdered sugar.

CRULLERS.—*Mrs. Wm. Alexander.*

1 cup buttermilk, 2 cups sugar, 2 eggs, 1 teaspoon soda, ½ cup shortening, and flour enough to roll out easily. Cook same as doughnuts.

FRITTERS.—*Mrs. W. Fraser.*

1 pint sweet milk, 4 eggs, 1 quart flour, 3 teaspoons baking powder; fry in fat and serve hot with maple syrup.

DRUGS

...Inman & Son...

You Want { The best Drugs or none. / The best Drugs at the lowest prices.

We Give you Both.

PRESCRIPTIONS Accurately compounded day or night.

FLAVORING EXTRACTS — Our own make { They're pure, / That's sure.

LAXATIVE ANTI-GRIPPE CAPSULES — Cure a cold in one day.

Our Motto { If it's from Inman's / it's good.

COR. FOURTH AND C STS.

Kodaks and Supplies.

Telephone Red 35.

MRS. M. COIT

San Rafael. Cal.

—— Milliner ——

Dealer in

Fourth Street, Between C and D.

Velvets, Satins, Flowers, Laces, Feathers, Tissues and Ruching. Dressmakers' Supplies. Hosiery, Mourning Goods, Etc.

ALEX. SHEVITS

San Rafael.

Dealer in

Ladies' and Gents' **Fine Shoes**

Full Line of Gents' Furnishing Goods. Boys' and Girls' School Shoes a Specialty. All Goods at S. F. prices.

Cor. Fourth below C St.   San Rafael

Pastry and Pies.

PASTRY.—*Mrs. Geo. M. Dodge.*

Into 1 cup flour rub 1 tablespoon lard; then wet it with enough ice-cold water to make a soft dough. Roll out and spread with little bits of butter all over. Then sprinkle lightly with flour, and fold over into a roll. Roll out again with rolling pin and spread again with lard. Then repeat as first time, and roll in bits of butter the third time. If this method is followed and ice water is used, and if the dough is handled lightly and quickly, a nice flaky crust will be obtained.

PIE CRUST.—*Mrs. Geo. Bunn.*

3½ cups of flour, 1 cup of shortening (half butter and half lard), a scant cup of water very cold, a pinch of salt. Handle as little as possible.

PIE CRUST.—*Mrs. L. A. Lancel.*

¾ of a pint of flour, 2 heaping tablespoons lard, 1 teaspoon yeast powder, 2 eggs. Mix in a bowl with cold water until the dough is ready to roll out, not too stiff; roll out into a thin sheet, spread lard or butter over it and a little dusting of flour; then roll together; repeat this 3 times; cover a plate, fill and bake. Spread a little lard on the top crust when it is put into the oven.

LEMON PIE.—*Mrs. A. A. Curtis.*

Yolks of 4 eggs, 1 cup sugar, juice of 3 lemons, whites of 2 eggs. Whip the whites, and mix with the yolks, sugar and lemon juice; cook all together in the mush boiler until thick, stirring all the time. Put this filling in the pie crust which should be baked first; whip the whites of 4 eggs for the top; and set in oven for a few seconds. Very fine.

LEMON PIE.—*Mrs. W. F. C. Hasson.*

Beat to a cream 4 ounces butter and 2 cups of sugar; add grated rind of 1 lemon, and the yolks of 10 eggs well beaten; mix in thoroughly lime juice enough to make quite sour, line a dish with rich paste and bake it. Pour in the mixture and bake in a moderate oven till quite firm, say 10 or 12 minutes. Then spread over it the whites of 3 eggs beaten to a very stiff froth with 2 tablespoons sugar and a little lemon; smooth carefully and put back in the oven till a light brown. Serve at once.

LEMON PIES.—*Mrs. W. F. Jones.*

1 tablespoon corn starch wet in a little cold water; pour over this about a teacup of boiling water; when clear it ought to be pretty thick; then add ¾ cup of sugar, 1 tablespoon butter, the grated rind and juice

PASTRY AND PIES.

of 1 lemon, and the yolks of 3 eggs. Line your pan with nice rich crust and bake, then pour in the filling. Beat the 3 whites to a stiff froth, add a few drops of lemon extract and 6 heaping tablespoons powdered sugar. Place in the oven for a few moments until a light brown.

PINEAPPLE PIE.—*Mrs. F. M. Angellotti.*

1 cup grated pineapple, 1 cup sugar, 1 cup cream, 1 tablespoon butter, 3 eggs (only the yolks); mix and bake about 45 minutes. Use the 3 whites of eggs for meringue.

VINEGAR PIE.—*Mrs. Prodtrottea.*

5 eggs, 2 large cups boiling water, 5 tablespoons vinegar, about 5 tablespoons corn starch, butter size of an egg, 1 cup of sugar. Put the water, sugar, butter and vinegar in a pan, thicken with cornstarch, then add the beaten yolks, flavor with lemon and pour into the crust (bake the crust first); beat the whites of the eggs with 4 tablespoons of sugar, put over the pies, and set into the oven to brown lightly. This will make 2 pies.

CUSTARD PIE.—*Mrs. E. B. Mahon.*

3 eggs, 2 tablespoons of sugar, 1 pint of milk, nutmeg and a pinch of salt.

BANANA PIE, NO. 1.—*Mrs. A. A. Smith.*

Line a pan with good pastry; slice in very thinly 2 bananas; make a custard of 1 pint of milk, 2 well beaten eggs, a pinch of salt and 2 tablespoons of sugar; pour over the bananas, and bake as a custard pie.

BANANA PIE, NO. 2.—*Mrs. A. A. Smith.*

Make a banana pie with a lower crust only; bake the crust first, fill it with sliced bananas and powdered sugar; the fruit will soften in a few minutes; cover with whipped cream, and eat at once.

SQUASH PIES.—*Mrs. W. F. Jones.*

Line the baking plates with nice, rich crust. Steam a Hubbard squash, and when done pass it through a colander. For 2 pies, beat up 4 eggs, add 1 pint of squash, a little salt, 1 cup of sugar, 1 heaping teaspoon ginger, and ¾ of a quart of milk. Bake until the mixture sets. 1 cup of cream in place of some of the milk is a great improvement.

LEMON CHEESE CAKES.—*Mrs. V. Neale.*

Ingredients: ½ pound butter, 1 pound lump sugar, 6 eggs, rind of 2 lemons, juice of 3. Put all in saucepan, having carefully strained the juice of lemons and grated the rind. Keep stirring over fire till as thick as honey, when it is done. (Will keep in jars for 3 months). Line some patty pans with good puff paste, rather more than half fill them with the mixture, and bake in 15 or 20 minutes in good brisk oven.

SWEDISH APPLE CAKE.—*Miss A. Gordon.*

Roll out some rich pie paste, brush the edge with yolk of egg, and let it bake at a medium heat. Peel 6 apples, cut them into small pieces, and mix them with 1½ ounces of sugar; cook until quite soft; mix with them ½ ounce of finely shredded orange peel, and the same of burnt almonds; add a little cinnamon and some grated lemon, and spread this mixture upon the paste. Beat up the whites of 2 eggs to snow. Mix in 2¼ ounces of sugar, and put this into a conical, rolled paper bag; squeeze a network as well as a wreath-like edge on the cake; dust it with sugar, and put it in to the oven until it is a pale golden color.

ORANGE TARTLETS.—*Mrs. C. F. Robinson.*

3 large fine oranges (juice of 3 and rind 1), 1 cup sugar, 2 dessert-spoons butter, juice of ½ a lemon, 3 teaspoons cornstarch wet with lemon juice and 2 tablespoons of water, 1 egg; beat to a smooth cream and let it boil up, then pour into patty tins lined with crust, and bake.

FIG PUFFS.—*Miss Margaret B emner.*

1 pound figs cut in small pieces, 1 cup of water, ½ cup of sugar; boil the figs until tender; add the sugar while boiling; let cool; make a good rich pie crust, roll out a piece, spread the figs on, then roll out another piece about the same size and thin, and turn over the figs cut in bars 1½ inches wide and 4 inches long; bake in a quick oven. These are very good.

MINCE MEAT.—*Mrs. Carter P. Pomeroy.*

(From an old English recipe handed down in the Morris family.)

1 beef's tongue well boiled, skinned and chopped fine; 2 pounds of beef suet and 8 pounds of tart apples, both chopped fine; 1 pint of molasses, 3 pounds of sugar, 4 tablespoons of cinnamon, 2 nutmegs, 2 tablespoons cloves, a little salt sprinkled on the tongue; 1 quart of rich boiled cider (which should be boiled down till it is as thick as syrup)—1 quart after boiling. Put everything together and set over a kettle of boiling water till the suet melts; then add 4 pounds of raisins stoned, ½ pound of citron cut very small, and 2 pounds of currants. Wine or brandy if you like, and more sugar if you like it sweeter.

GENERAL DIRECTIONS FOR MAKING MINCE MEAT. —*Mrs. W. F. Jones.*

Boil 1 fresh beef tongue and 1 beef heart until tender, in as little water as possible, and salt well when half done. Lean beef can be used, but is not so nice, for it is apt to be fibrous. Prepare the heart and tongue, and chop very fine. Measure, and use twice as many chopped apples as meat, and ½ as much chopped suet as meat. 1 quart of boiled cider, or 1 gallon of cider boiled down to a quart; 1 quart syrup from sweet pickles, that from clingstone peaches is best; 1 pint of best brandy; the grated rind and juice of 3 lemons; 2 nutmegs, 2 tablespoons cloves, 2 tablespoons cinnamon, salt, 4 pounds seeded raisins, 2 pounds currants washed thoroughly, 1 pound citron chopped fine; brown sugar and syrup to taste. Cook all together in a preserving pan, stirring frequently. If too dry, add more syrup or pickle juice. More spices can also be added if liked. Put hot in fruit jars and this will keep indefinitely. When making the pies, add a tablespoon of brandy or wine to each pie.

This is the Brand

Each case contains 3 doz. 1 lb packages.

Each package makes three pies.

LIBBY, McNEIL & LIBBY, are the packers

We are the agents

ASK YOUR GROCER FOR IT

Dodge, Sweeney & Co. San Francisco

SCOTT & CO.

San Rafael Cal.

Hardware Merchants

Gordon Block, Fourth St. Paints and Oils, Hardware, Crockery, Carpenters' Tools . . . .
Bet. C and D Sts., San Rafael.

P. E. DUFFY

San Rafael, Cal.

Proprietor . . **Bay View Carriage Factory**

Firstclass Workmen, and Firstclass Work. Washers, Rubbers, Etc. Always on hand. All kinds of Carriage Work done on short notice

Corner of **THIRD AND C STS.**

Pickles, Catsups, Etc.

OIL CUCUMBER PICKLE.—*Miss Parsons, Tamalpais.*

100 small cucumbers the size of a finger, sliced across in quarters; 1 quart small onions (1 inch in diameter) sliced very thin. Put the above into a colander in layers, sprinkling in ¼ pint of salt. Put on them a heavy weight and let drain 6 hours. Put into a large pan the following: 8 tablespoons of olive oil, 1 tablespoon of celery seed, 1 dessertspoon of black pepper; mix well, toss in the cucumbers and onions, and mix again. Pack in Mason jars, fill with cold vinegar, and seal (without cooking). Makes about 5 pints.

OIL PICKLES.—*Mrs. J. L. Tharp.*

50 small cucumbers and 200 button onions sliced; put in a colander, cover with salt, and a plate with weight on it. Let stand 24 hours. Mix with it, 1 ounce celery seed, ½ ounce white mustard seed and ½ ounce black, 1 cup sweet oil. Put in jars and cover with vinegar.

FOR TWO GALLONS OF PICKLES.—*Mrs. W. F. Jones.*

Put 2 gallons of small cucumbers in salt and water for 3 days; then wash thoroughly, and put in a jar. Boil 2 quarts of vinegar with a teacup of whole mustard, a handful each of cloves, allspice and black pepper, and a teacup of broken cinnamon all tied in a thin bag; to this add 1 pound of brown sugar. With the pickles put a few pods of red pepper and roots of horseradish; pour the vinegar over the pickles, and if it does not cover them add more vinegar and let the bag of spices remain in the jar. Scald the vinegar every day for 5 days; then pour 1 coffee cup of molasses over the top and let it gradually settle down.

MUSTARD PICKLES.—*Miss Tena Bremner.*

1 quart large cucumbers chopped, 1 quart small ones left whole, 1 quart large onions chopped, 1 quart small ones whole, 1 large cauliflower pulled apart, 3 strong peppers chopped fine, 3 small ones left whole. Put all in separate dishes and cover with hot brine; cover closely to keep steam in; let stand over night; in the morning drain them and put all together, adding 3 cups sugar, ½ gallon vinegar, ¼ pound white mustard, ¼ ounce celery seed; put all in a kettle and scald them. Make a paste of ¾ cup of flour, 3 ounces yellow mustard, ½ ounce turmeric powder mixed with a little vinegar; turn this in slowly, stir briskly and let it boil up; then bottle.

SWEET PICKLES.—*Mrs. Geo. Bunn.*

3½ pounds brown sugar, 1 quart vinegar, 2 tablespoons each of cloves, allspice and cinnamon in small bags. Boil the syrup and spices;

when boiling hot pour it over 7 pounds of fruit; let stand 24 hours; pour off, boil again, and scald again as many times as necessary, according to size of fruit; for peaches about 4 times is sufficient; for smaller fruits, such as grapes or plums, 2 or 3 times will answer.

CHOW-CHOW.—*Mrs. Robert E. Neil.*

12 large cucumbers, 4 large or 8 medium onions, 2 heads cauliflower, ½ peck green tomatoes cut in small pieces, 1 quart string beans (white wax beans are best)—string as for cooking, and break once; 3 large red peppers cut in strips, 50 small cucumbers about 2 inches long used whole, 2 quarts small silver onions, peeled and used whole. Pack all down in salt over night. In the morning wash off the salt, and drain well in a colander. Then boil in 1½ gallons of good cider vinegar, adding 1 pound brown sugar, 2 ounces white mustard, 1 ounce celery seed whole. Into 1 pint cold vinegar thoroughly mix 1 small box yellow ground mustard, 4 tablespoons ground black pepper, 1 horseradish root grated, and 2 ounces turmeric; add to the boiling liquid, and boil all together from 2½ to 3 hours. Put into glass or stone jars, while still warm.

GREEN TOMATO PICKLE.—*Mrs. A. E. Menzies.*

4 quarts green tomatoes after having been chopped, 2 roots horseradish, 1 small teacup salt, 1 teacup black mustard seed, 1 teacup white mustard seed, 2 tablespoons black pepper, 2 red peppers (without seeds), 2 or 3 celery stalks, 1 cup onions (or same of nasturtiums), 1 teaspoon each of cloves, mace and cinnamon, 2 cups brown sugar, 3 pints strong vinegar. Chop the tomatoes, sprinkle with salt called for in recipe, and drain for 12 hours; if onions are used, let them drain with tomatoes. Boil for 1 hour; add the horseradish and celery later so that they only boil ½ hour. Before closing the jars, fill to the brim with hot vinegar.

CHOW-CHOW.—*Mrs. W. F. Jones.*

25 cents' worth of green tomatoes and 10 cents' worth of green cucumbers, sliced and sprinkled with about 2 cups of salt; let them stand over night; in the morning wash thoroughly and cook until tender in equal parts of vinegar and water; when tender drain, and throw away the liquid. Slice 10 cents' worth of dry onions and 1 dozen bell peppers, and put them to cook in 3 quarts of vinegar; when tender drain off the vinegar, and return to the stove for the sauce. To the vinegar add ½ cup of ground mustard, 2 tablespoons of black pepper, 1 cup of flour wet in a little of the vinegar, 4 cups of brown sugar, 1 tablespoon celery seed. Cook all until the sauce thickens, and pour it over the chow-chow. Put in the jars while hot, and seal. In this way it keeps for years. Delicious.

PICCALILLI.—*Mrs. W. J. Wickman.*

1 peck green tomatoes, 8 large onions chopped fine, 1 cup of salt well stirred in. Let it stand over night and in the morning drain off all the liquor, add 2 quarts of water and 1 quart of vinegar; boil all together 20 minutes. Drain all through a sieve or colander, put it back into the kettle again, turn over it 2 quarts of vinegar, 1 pound of sugar, ½ pint of white mustard seed, 2 tablespoons of ground pepper, 2 of cinnamon,

1 of cloves, 2 of ginger, and 1 of allspice, and ½ teaspoon of cayenne pepper. Boil all together 15 minutes or until tender. Stir it often to prevent scorching. Seal in glass jars. A good relish with meat or fish.

PICKLED EGGS.—*Mrs. W. J. Wickman.*

3 dozen eggs boiled hard; drop in cold water, remove the shells, and pack them when entirely cold in a wide-mouthed jar large enough to let them in or out without breaking. Take as much vinegar as will cover them entirely, and boil in it white pepper, allspice, and a little root ginger: pour this over the eggs in the jar, occasionally putting in a tablespoon of white and black mustard seed mixed, a small piece of race ginger, a garlic if liked, horseradish ungrated, whole cloves, and a very little allspice. Slice 2 or 3 green peppers and add in very small quantities. They will be fit for use in 8 or 10 days.

TOMATO CATSUP.—*Miss Parsons, Tamalpais.*

2 quarts of tomatoes skinned and chopped, 1½ pints vinegar, ½ pound brown sugar, ⅔ pint New Orleans molasses, 1 teaspoon red pepper, 2 tablespoons salt, 2 onions (2 inches in diameter) chopped fine, 3 tablespoons winter squash steamed and mashed. Mix all together and boil down to ½ the original quantity. Excellent. Makes about 3 quarts.

TOMATO CATSUP.—*Mrs. A. A. Smith.*

Scald and strain tomatoes through a sieve to remove seeds and skins; then add to each gallon of juice 3 tablespoons of salt, 4 of ground mustard, 3 of black pepper, 2 of allspice, 2 of cinnamon, 1 of cloves, 1 teaspoon of cayenne pepper, 1 pint of white wine vinegar; simmer slowly for 4 hours, bottle and cork tight.

APPLE CATSUP.—*Miss Tena Bremner.*

Stew apples in as little water as possible, and to 7 cups of pulp add 1½ cups sugar, 1 teaspoon pepper, 1 teaspoon cloves, 1 teaspoon cinnamon, 1 teaspoon ginger, and 2 medium-sized onions chopped very fine. Beat well together, and then add 1 tablespoon salt and 1 cup vinegar. Stir well until all the ingredients are blended, then boil 1 hour and bottle while hot. Fill top of jar with vinegar to exclude air and prevent mould.

CHILI SAUCE.—*Mrs. J. L. Tharp.*

8 large tomatoes, 4 large Chili peppers, 4 red peppers, 1 large onion, 1 tablespoon of sugar, 1 of ginger, 1 of cloves, 1 of allspice, 1 of salt, 2 cups of vinegar. Boil down to half the quantity.

CHILI SAUCE.—*Mrs. W. F. Jones.*

12 large ripe tomatoes pared, 2 large onions, 4 bell peppers, 1 tablespoon salt, 4 tablespoons sugar, and 2 teacups vinegar; chop the onions and peppers fine, put all together in a kettle, and let them simmer about 2 hours when it should be quite thick. If one likes a hotter sauce, use the long peppers; but I prefer the flavor of the others.

SPICED CURRANTS.—*Mrs. J. L. Tharp.*

5 pounds picked currants, 4 pounds sugar, 1 pint of vinegar, ½ table-

spoon ground cloves, ½ tablespoon allspice, ½ tablespoon cinnamon, 1 dozen whole cloves. Put all together and boil ¾ of an hour.

SPICED CURRANTS.—*Mrs. W. F. Jones.*

5 pounds of currants, 4 pounds of sugar, 1 pint of vinegar, 1 tablespoon ground cloves, 2 tablespoons cinnamon; cook all until quite rich. To make Currant Soy pass the mixture through a sieve, and cook until thick.

FRENCH MUSTARD.—*Miss L. P. Trumbull.*

1 egg, 1 teaspoon butter, 2 heaping tablespoons sugar, 1 teaspoon salt, 3 heaping tablespoons mustard, ⅔ cup vinegar and a speck of cayenne pepper. Beat the egg, dissolve the mustard in a little vinegar, and add the other ingredients; put in a double boiler or in a bowl over the teakettle, and stir until it thickens. This will keep a long time.

TO PICKLE OLIVES.—*Mrs. W. F. Jones.*

Dissolve a 1-pound can of Babbitt's Potash in 5 gallons of water. Wash the olives and put in only enough to have the lye simply cover them. Stir every few hours and taste. When the bitter is almost gone (the time varying from 24 hours to 9 days), pour off the lye and soak in clear cold water, changing frequently until the lye taste is all gone, but the olives must not get soft or mushy. Make a brine of 14 ounces of salt to a gallon of water, and pour it cold over the olives. Bottle cold, filling the bottles well. I have excellent results preserving ripe olives by this recipe.

ADVERTISEMENTS.

HARDING & REILLY

Matt. Reilly
George Harding

Practical Horseshoers

Telphone Black 21

Particular attention given to trotting horses, flesh foundering, quarter cracks, pigeon toeing, knee sprung, overreaching . .

THIRD STREET,
Bet. B and C.

H. A. GORLEY

San Rafael
Cal.

Dealer in

Foreign and Domestic Dry Goods Clothing

Hats and caps,
Rubber Goods, at City prices

Gents' Furnishing Goods

809 and 811 Fourth St.

The Oldest and most reliable dry goods house in San Rafael.

E. H. CONWAY

Telephone
Red 21

Plumbing and Gas=Fitting

STOVES OF ALL KINDS
KITCHEN UTENSILS

San Rafael, Cal.

**B STREET
BET. SECOND
AND THIRD.**

A. B. THOMSON

Linens imported from Europe direct   San Rafael

Jellies and Fruits.

Rules.

Make all jellies or preserves in granite or porcelain pans.

Fruit for jelly should be not quite ripe.

Fill the jars, run a knife to the bottom and then around the edge, that the air bubbles may rise.

Have the fruit hot, fill the jars full, screw the covers tight (the rubber rings must be new each year); to test the tightness of the covers, turn the jars upside down and let them so remain for several hours.

Boiling jelly after the sugar is in makes it dark in color.

Fruit steamed in the jar, and a syrup poured over it afterwards, is nicest.

CURRANT JELLY.—*Mrs. W. F. Jones.*

Cook the currants on the stems, after they have been carefully picked over; put into a bag and let drain; measure and return to the fire and boil 15 minutes; then add an equal quantity of granulated sugar warmed in the oven, and boil 5 minutes longer; pour into glasses. If the flavor of raspberries is liked, cook with the currants about 2 little baskets of raspberries to 1 small drawer of currants. After using the juice that drained off, squeeze the bag and make jelly which will not be so clear but does well for puddings and cakes. Skim thoroughly as it boils.

QUINCE JELLY.—*Mrs. W. F. Jones.*

Wipe the quinces carefully, then quarter them, removing nothing but the blows or any imperfect part, put on in just sufficient cold water to cover the fruit; cook until tender, stirring from the bottom carefully, but do not break the fruit, or the juice will not run. Drain through a bag and squeeze (for this jelly will be clear if squeezed, and much more juice will be obtained); measure and return to the fire and boil from $\frac{1}{2}$ to 1 hour according to whether the juice is watery or rich; add an equal amount of sugar which has been heated in the oven, and boil until it begins to jelly around the pan or drops from the spoon. Skim carefully. Jelly can be made from the cores and rinds left from making preserves. In making preserves steam the fruit until a little tender, then pour the syrup over, and the fruit will not be leathery.

GRAPE JELLY.—*Mrs. W. F. Jones.*

Wash the grapes (Isabellas are the best); pick from the stem, and proceed as in currant jelly. To prevent crystals forming after the jelly gets a little old, cook a small proportion of juicy apples, as you cook quinces, and add their juice to the grape juice. The apples also help to make a firmer jelly. Proceed as in other jelly, cooking about 1 hour before adding the sugar.

TO KEEP JELLY FROM MOULDING.—*Mrs. W. F. Jones.*

Cover the jelly with thin brown paper; then melt in a saucepan some paraffine and pour over the paper to the depth of a quarter of an inch, and pour back into the saucepan immediately from the jelly glass; it will leave a thin coating over the top which will keep the jelly perfectly. I have used this with good success for many years.

QUINCE HONEY.—*Miss A. Gordon.*

5 nice quinces pared and grated, 1 pint of water, 5 pounds of granulated sugar; stir the grated quinces into the boiling sugar and water; cook 15 minutes, pour into glasses, and let cool before covering.

RHUBARB SAUCE.—*Miss H. Pregge.*

Cut up the rhubarb into small pieces, leaving all the tender skin on; then put into a double boiler with sugar enough to sweeten, and cook until tender. This is very nice.

CRANBERRY SAUCE.—*Mrs. W. F. Jones.*

Put 1 quart of well picked cranberries into 1 pint of boiling water, and boil rapidly until done; then press through a colander, return to the fire, add 2 cups of sugar, and cook a short time. The flavor is more delicate when it is brought to a half-jellied consistency.

ORANGE MARMALADE.—*Mrs. Carter P. Pomeroy.*

Slice 1 dozen oranges skins and all, with a potato slicer (the kind that comes for Saratoga potatoes); weigh the sliced fruit, and to each pound add 1½ pints of water and boil for ¾ of an hour; then let it stand for 24 hours; weigh it again, and to each pound add 1½ pounds of sugar and the juice of 1 lemon, and boil for 25 minutes, not longer. Use common sour oranges, taking out the seeds as you slice them. Delicious and very easy to make.

ORANGE MARMALADE.—*Mrs. Oliver*

6 pounds bitter oranges, 6 pounds sugar; peel the oranges and boil the skins till tender; rub the inside of each orange through a sieve to keep back the seeds; put the pulp and skins with the sugar, and boil half an hour.

ORANGE MARMALADE.—*Mrs. W. F. Jones.*

Take about 2 dozen nice juicy oranges, grate the rind of half of them and pare the other half. Cook the parings until tender, in plenty of water, throwing away the water. Carefully separate the seeds and white part from the juice and pulp. When the skins are well cooked, remove all the white coating inside, and clip the rind with scissors into fine strips. Measure or weigh both the rind and pulp, and put it on to boil for about an hour; then add the same amount of heated sugar, and let this boil until the right consistency is reached, stirring constantly. It can be tested by putting a little in a saucer on ice or in any cool place.

KELLY BROS.

Telephone Red 13

The · · Leading Plumbers
•••

And Dealers in

Plumbing Supplies, Tinware, Oils, Hardware, Agateware, Garden Hose, Bicycles, Electric Supplies. Stoves, Paints,

---

R. MAGNES

Established 1878.

Dealer in

Boots and Shoes
Gents' Furnishing Goods

DRY GOODS, CLOTHING AND HATS

Opera House Block,
Fourth St. bet. C and D
San Rafael

Buying my goods for cash, I can and do sell cheaper than anyone else.

EUGENE W. SMITH

San Rafael

Practical Shoemaker

⚜ ⚜

Ladies' and Children's Shoes a Specialty
All work promptly attended to . . . .
REPAIRING DONE.

B St. bet. 3rd and 4th

Phillips Wire Fence

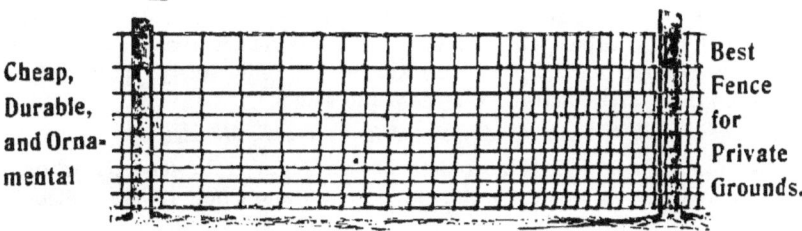

Cheap, Durable, and Ornamental

Best Fence for Private Grounds.

The wire work costs from 4 to 15 cents per running foot according to the mesh.

W. N. ROSS,
Agent Marin Co.

Confectionery.

CREAM CANDY.—*Miss Tena Bremner.*

2 cups granulated sugar, ½ cup cold water, ¼ teaspoon cream of tartar, 1 teaspoon vanilla, almond, or any flavoring desired. Boil sugar, cream of tartar and water together until it hairs from the spoon; add the flavoring; set it in a cool place, and when nearly cold beat it until light and creamy; when cold enough to handle, mold into any shapes desired; place on a platter to harden. Melt unsweetened chocolate in a double boiler, and with a long pin dip the creams into the chocolate and set aside to cool. A nice variety may be made by removing the pits from dates, and filling with plain cream shaped to fit, or with cream into which chopped nuts have been mixed. Almonds blanched and placed on the creams before they are quite cool, or walnuts halved and creams put between them, make a variety.

FRENCH CREAM CANDY.—*Mrs McMahon.*

5 cups of granulated sugar, 2 cups of water, ¼ teaspoon of cream of tartar; stir all together, then put on the stove and boil without stirring about an hour, until it threads; with a wet cloth, constantly wipe around the edge to prevent it from going to sugar. When done, put the pan in cold water to cool, not letting it get too cold; when cool beat it until stiff, then knead it on a marble slab until all lumps are out; flavor and work into creams.

MAPLE CREAM.—*Mrs J. L. Tharp.*

2 cups of maple sugar, ½ cup of cream, ¼ cup almonds blanched and chopped. Boil until crisp in water. Put in the nuts after taking from the fire, stirring until cool.

PEANUT CANDY.—*Mrs. W. F. Jones.*

Prepare 1 pint of shelled peanuts in a square pan, rubbing off all the skins. Put 2 cups of granulated sugar over the fire dry, and stir constantly until melted; then pour it over the candy. Great care must be used to prevent the sugar from burning.

PANACHE CANDY.—*Mrs. Oliver.*

4 cups brown sugar, 1 cup milk, the meats of 2 pounds of walnuts broken, 1 large tablespoon vanilla; boil all together over a slow fire till it sugars around the edge of the kettle; stir constantly; pour into a buttered dish, and cut into squares while warm.

TOFFEE CANDY.—*Miss Agnes I. Menzies.*

2 cups of sugar, 2 tablespoons brown sugar, 1 tablespoon water, 1 tablespoon any flavoring preferred. It is done when it has boiled 20 minutes.

CONFECTIONERY.

MOLASSES CANDY.—*Miss May Dollar.*

1 cup of molasses, 3 tablespoons of brown sugar, 1 tablespoon of butter, 2 tablespoons of vinegar: boil 20 minutes; flavor as you like; make it with New Orleans molasses.

CHOCOLATE CARAMELS.—*Miss May Dollar.*

1 cup of molasses, ½ cup of white sugar, ¼ pound of chocolate, 1 heaping tablespoon of butter; boil until hard, then pour into buttered plates, and when hard, cut into squares. Stir while boiling.

VANILLA CREAM TAFFY.—*Hoover.*

Weigh 4 pounds of white sugar; place it in a kettle; add to this 2 tablespoons of vinegar, 1 pint of rich cream and 2 ounces of butter; set the kettle on a moderate fire, and stir and cook the batch to a slight crack; pour out on buttered plates or a marble slab, and let it become cool enough to handle; then pull the batch, and flavor with 1 teaspoon of vanilla extract, when it will be ready for use.

TAFFY.—*Miss Agnes I. Menzies.*

3 cups brown sugar, 1 tablespoon molasses, 1½ tablespoons butter, 1 tablespoon cream, a pinch of cream of tartar; flavor with vanilla; put in a buttered pan large enough to make the candy thin. Stir all the time.

TO PREPARE SALTED ALMONDS.—*Miss A. Gordon.*

Blanch them by pouring hot water on them. When they are blanched and dry, measure them, and over each cupful of nuts pour 1 tablespoon of best olive oil; then sprinkle with a tablespoon of salt for each cupful of nuts, mixing thoroughly. Put in not too hot an oven for about 10 minutes, or until they are nicely browned.

SALTED ALMONDS.—*Mrs. W. F. Jones.*

I have tried salting almonds in the oven, in butter, in olive oil, by sprinkling them over night with salt and roasting dry; but I find the most satisfactory way is to heat a little olive oil in a very small saucepan, drop a few of the almonds in and fry them as I would doughnuts. When brown, skim them out, throw them on brown paper and sprinkle with salt. As long as the olive oil is not burned, it can be used again by adding a little more oil to it.

GO TO HOOVER'S

for ...

Fine Candies

Ice Cream Soda
a Specialty

SALTED ALMONDS.   FRUIT ICES TO ORDER.

KINSELLA & JOHNSON

Agents Rochester Lamps.

Dealers in

Hardware

And all kinds of

HOUSE

FURNISHING

GOODS

PLUMBING

AND

GAS-FITTING

B Street, bet. Third and Fourth.   Telephone Red 31.

Drinks.

ORANGEADE.—*Hoover.*

To 1 quart of iced water add 4 ounces of dry granulated sugar, the juice of 2 lemons and 3 oranges; mix thoroughly together until all the sugar is dissolved, when it will be ready to serve. A good summer drink.

RASPBERRY SHRUB.—*Mrs. J. E. Alexander.*

Cover the raspberries with best vinegar, and let them lay over night. In the morning mash the berries and squeeze through a coarse bag. To every pint of juice add 1 pint of sugar. Boil 20 minutes. When cool, bottle. This will make quite a thick syrup, which must be diluted when drank.

RASPBERRY VINEGAR.—*Mrs. J. M. Dollar.*

Put 4 quarts of red raspberries into an earthen or granite vessel; cover with good vinegar, and let stand for 24 hours; scald and strain; add 1 pound of sugar to every pint of juice; boil for about 20 minutes; skim well, and bottle.

CURRANT AND RASPBERRY SYRUP.—*Mrs. J. M. Dollar.*

Take 8 pounds of very ripe red currants, pick off all the stems, and put them into a wide earthen pan; then squeeze them until the juice is all crushed out; leave them in the pan with the juice for 24 hours. Put 2 pounds of raspberries in a saucepan with 2 teacups of water, and boil them for a few minutes until they are all crushed; then squeeze all through a jelly bag or hair sieve, pressing well to get all the juice out; weigh the juice, and for every pound put 2 pounds of loaf sugar broken into pieces. Put the sugar into a preserving kettle with 1 pint of water, pour all the juice on it, let it boil for ½ hour, stirring frequently; then put it into small bottles and cork it for use. 2 tablespoonfuls in a glass of water makes a very refreshing drink in summer. Cherry syrup may be made in the same way with Morella cheries.

NECTAR CREAM.—*Miss L. P. Trumbull.*

2 quarts boiling water, 3½ pounds white sugar, 4 ounces tartaric acid, whites of 6 eggs, 2 ounces wintergreen essence or any other preferred. Put sugar in water, and boil 10 minutes, then the acid and let it boil up; let it stand till milk-warm; beat the eggs stiff, stir them in with the wintergreen, and put in bottles; Mix 2 tablespoons of this cream in a glass of water, with a wee bit of soda; beat and drink.

RHUBARB WATER.—*Mrs. J. M. Dollar.*

Cut up about 6 or 8 sticks of rhubard without peeling (wash well first), put into a stewpan, add 1 quart water, and boil for about 15 minutes; then strain into a pitcher, and add sugar and lemon juice. When cold it is fit for use.

BLACKBERRY CORDIAL.—*Mrs. R. E. Neil.*

2 quarts blackberry juice, 2 pounds granulated sugar, ¼ ounce cinnamon, ¼ ounce cloves, ¼ ounce allspice; simmer 20 minutes; when cold add 1 pint of the best brandy; then bottle and seal tight.

CHOCOLATE.—*Miss H. Pregge.*

With 4 tablespoons of grated chocolate mix 1 of sugar, and wet with 1 of boiling water; rub this smooth with the bowl of the spoon, and then stir it into 1 pint of boiling water; let this boil up once; then add 1 pint of good milk; let this boil up again, and serve. A spoonful of whipped cream put on top of each cupful is quite an improvement.

G. W. CLARK & CO.

J. B. Stanford
T. J. Stack

IMPORTERS AND JOBBERS

Foreign and American **Wall Paper**

• Interior Decorators •

and manufacturers of

WINDOW SHADES

653 Market St.
San Francisco, Cal.

WM. SALE

Pianos for sale and to Rent.

Furniture, Carpets, Upholstery

Paper Hangings, Picture Frames, Spring Beds, Mattresses, Pillows

⚜

ALL KINDS OF PLAIN AND FANCY FURNITURE MADE TO ORDER.

608 Fourth Street
San Rafael

Marin Co. Furniture Warehouse
Order by Telephone.

Fine Carpetings,

Elegant Upholstery,

Rich Furniture.

Chas. M. Plum & Co.

Upholstery Company,

1301 to 1307 Market Street,   Cor. Ninth, S. F

Foods for the Sick.

BEEF TEA.—*Mrs. D. Whittemore.*

RULES.—1. Never let beef tea boil. 2. Always begin with cold water. 3. The finer the beef is cut the better. 4. There should be no fat, gristle or bone. 5. The proportion of beef and water is 1 pint of water to 1 pound of meat. 6. After being carefully made, remove all fat from the surface after it gets cold.

Put 1 pound of beef into a glass fruit jar with 1 pint of cold water; let it soak for 2 hours; screw on the top and then set the jar into a vessel of boiling water, and boil for 3 hours; strain and salt to taste. The last vestige of fat can be removed with a piece of white blotting paper.

MUTTON BROTH.—*Mrs. D. Whittemore.*

1½ pounds lean mutton, 1 quart of cold water, salt to taste. Cut the mutton into thin slices, let it simmer in the cold water for 1 hour; then let it boil for 1 hour longer, and strain the broth through a sieve. This may be thickened with a little sago, if desired; or may be eaten with toasted crackers. This broth is more nourishing than beef tea.

OATMEAL GRUEL.—*Mrs. D. Whittemore.*

1 cup oatmeal, 2 quarts water, ½ teaspoon salt. Boil slowly until reduced to 1 quart; strain, and thin with milk if desired.

CORN MEAL GRUEL.—*Mrs. D. Whittemore.*

1 cup corn meal, 1 quart water, 1 pinch salt. Make a thin paste of cornmeal, mashing out all the lumps; stir it into the boiling water, and let it boil ¾ of an hour, being very careful it does not burn. Corn meal gruel must always be well cooked.

ALBUMEN WATER.—*Mrs. D. Whittemore.*

½ pint of cold water, whites of 2 eggs, 1 teaspoon sugar of milk. Drop the whites of the eggs into the water, stir gently until well mixed, then sweeten; give cold. A valuable aid in nourishing a child when sick with diarrhea.

UNLEAVENED WAFERS.—*Mrs. D. Whittemore.*

Mix 1 quart of flour into a stiff dough with sweet milk into which a little salt has been stirred; roll out very thin, cut into round cakes, roll these out again very thin; bake quickly. These wafers are easily digested and are very delicate.

TONIC.—*Miss Kate O'Neill.*

Yolk of 1 egg, 1 dessertspoon of best brandy, ½ glass of barley water, white of 1 egg. Beat well together the yolk of the egg and the dessertspoon of brandy; add ½ glass of barley water (boiled and strained), and season to taste. Then stir in slowly the well beaten white of the egg. Take a wineglassful night and morning.

Miscellaneous.

BOSTON HARD SOAP.

5 pints melted grease strained, 1 pound of Babbitt's Potash, 1 pint boiling water poured over the potash, 1 quart of cold water added to the above. When the potash cools, pour the grease into it, stir until thick, then set away until the next morning. Set it on the stove, and add 5 quarts of hot water; when melted add ¾ cup of powdered borax and same of sugar; let it simmer ½ hour; pour into dishes and let it stand until the next morning; then cut the soap into pieces and put away in a dry place for 6 months before using. In saving grease, save all kinds. Very good.

LINIMENT.—*Mrs. Robert Dollar.*

Equal quantities each of ether, oil of juniper, spirits of camphor and hartshorn.

TO REMOVE GRASS STAINS.

Dip the stained part in kerosene oil, and rub well between the fingers; then rub in clear cold water until the stains disappear.

TO REMOVE MILDEW.

1 ounce soap, 1 ounce starch, 1 ounce salt, the juice of 1 lemon; dip the spots in this mixture and lay on the grass in the sun.

TO REMOVE IRON RUST.

Wet the spots in lemon juice and salt, and lay in the sun. Repeat until the iron rust disappears.

Table of Weights or Measures.

(Selected.)

1 quart of sifted flour (well heaped)	weight 1 pound
1 " " unsifted flour	weight 1 pound 1 ounce
3 coffeecups sifted flour (level)	weight 1 pound
4 teacups " " "	" 1 "
1 pint soft butter (well packed)	" 1 "
2 teacups soft " " "	" 1 "
1½ pints powdered sugar	" 1 "
2 coffeecups " " (level)	" 1 "
2¾ teacups " " "	" 1 "
1 pint granulated " (heaped)	" 14 ounces
1½ coffeecups " " (level)	" 1 pound
2 teacups " " "	" 1 "
1 pint best brown "	" 13 ounces
1¾ coffeecups " " (level)	" 1 pound
2½ teacups " " "	" 1 "
2 tablespoons (well rounded) powdered sugar or flour	" 1 ounce
1 " " " soft butter	" 1 "
3 " sweet chocolate, grated	" 1 "

2 teaspoons (heaping) flour, sugar, or meal, equal 1 heaping tablespoon

Liquids.

1 pint contains 16 fluid ounces (4 gills).
1 teacupful equals 8 fluid ounces or 2 gills.
4 teaspoonfuls equal 1 tablespoonful.
2 teaspoonfuls equal 1 dessertspoonful.
4 teacupfuls equal 1 quart.
A common sized tumbler holds about ½ pint.

To Our Readers.

We would call attention to the advertisements that appear on these pages. Let us show these firms our appreciation by giving them, in turn, our patronage.

FINIS.

Contents.

	Page.
Bread	5–9
Soups,	15–18
Fish and Shellfish	23–28
Meats, Poultry, Game and Meats Rechauffe	34–43
Vegetables	49–51
Salads	55–57
Cheese	59–60
Eggs	62–64
Puddings	68–73
Light Desserts	78–85
Frozen Dainties	87–88
Cakes, Cookies, Doughnuts, Etc.	94–106
Pastry and Pies	110–112
Pickles, Catsups, etc.	114–117
Jellies and Fruits	119–120
Confectionery	122–123
Drinks	125–126
Foods for the Sick	128
Miscellaneous	131
Table of weights and measures	132

www.ingramcontent.com/pod-product-compliance
Lightning Source LLC
Chambersburg PA
CBHW031333160426
43196CB00007B/672